I0528946

The Shit People Say!

What Not to Say to People With Chronic Illness

Marie Ciampa

This book is dedicated to the people who never learned to keep their mouths shut. To the well-meaning but wildly inappropriate comments, the unsolicited advice, and the "concerned" remarks that made me laugh, cringe, and sometimes roll my eyes. You're all part of my story, whether you realise it or not.

ACKNOWLEDGEMENTS

I want to take a moment to acknowledge my mum and dad—two people who have shaped me in ways I'll never be able to fully put into words.

My mum was diagnosed with an autoimmune, Fibromyalgia, when I was quite young, so I grew up watching and learning from her. She taught me what it means to sit with pain, to keep pushing through, but also to recognise the moments when it's okay to stop and let myself *feel*—to momentarily sit in the frustration before picking myself back up. She showed me the balance between strength and vulnerability, and for that, I will always be grateful.

My dad is, without question, my greatest supporter in life. He taught me that even when things are hard, I am capable of *anything* I set my mind to. He demonstrated what it truly means to be loved and supported, setting the bar for how I expect to be treated by anyone who comes into my life.

Mum and Dad—you both shaped the person I am today. And for that, I couldn't be more thankful.

Contents

The Things People Say: Exploring the Absurdity of Unsolicited Opinions

Autobiographies tend to lean heavily on the dramatic side, exploring the lives of people who are far more important than I am. But that's not what I want this book to be. I don't need to write a sob story or make this a pity party about how tough life has been for me. Sure, I'll give some background context because I think it's necessary to explain where I've been. However, the real focus of this story isn't about how sick I feel or how difficult my life has been—it's about all the f**ed up things people have said to me along the way.

We've all had it happen—the well-meaning comments from people who think they're helping, or worse, the casual remarks that are just plain rude. Medical professionals, family members, coworkers, and sometimes even random strangers who don't know my name—everyone has had something to say about my illness or my life. And let's be clear: a lot of it has been totally out of line. There was a time when these comments would make me sad, and I'd wonder why people think it's okay to talk to someone like that. Over time, I've learned to find a certain kind of amusement in it. I look back and laugh now, even if it was painful at the time.

Alright, buckle up, because here are just a few of the *classic* comments I've heard over the years. You know, the ones that make you question humanity and wonder if people really think before they speak. These are the ones I *remember*—and trust me, there have been *plenty* more. I've had to leave some out, though, not because I don't want to roast them, but because, let's be real, some of those people will probably read this, and I'd prefer to avoid more dramatics and a severe lack of self-accountability. We all know that person who'd make a scene just to avoid acknowledging their own stupidity.

I've had doctors look at my medical charts and say things like, "Well, you look fine today!" as if a quick glance at me means they know what I'm dealing with. I've had well-meaning relatives tell me to "just exercise more" or "push through it," as if my condition is just a case of laziness. I've even had people say, "You don't look sick!"—as if there's a checklist for how a sick person is supposed to appear. And then there are the coworkers who "don't understand why I need to take time off" (not in my current occupation, just as a disclosure to any possible bosses that may read this) or strangers who feel entitled to comment on how I'm *really* doing, based purely on how I look that day.

It used to bother me—a lot. There were days when I would stew over a comment for hours, wondering why it was okay for people to assume they knew the first thing about my life. But the thing is, when you've heard it enough times, it starts to lose its sting. I, too, started seeing the absurdity in these remarks. How can someone tell me how I "should" feel when they don't even know the full story? How can people think that looking "fine" means I'm actually okay?

The thing is, I've come to find it all rather amusing in a dark, twisted way. The audacity of it all—the fact that people feel so comfortable making these assumptions about my life, my body, my struggles. Its comical, like being a character in a story that's written by people who don't actually understand the plot. Every now and then, hearing someone say something utterly ridiculous, I can't help but laugh. What else can you do?

Sure, I still have hard days—days when the comments hit a little too close to home or when I feel exhausted from constantly explaining myself. Nevertheless, I've learned to just shake my head and smile. There's a strange freedom in that. I've lived with these conditions for long enough to know that no one else can define what my life is like. No one can reduce me to their assumptions or casual comments. So, I laugh. I laugh because if I don't, I'll end up crying—and I've got better things to do than that.

Some Context

When I was fifteen, my life started to change in ways I couldn't fully understand at the time. It began with a feeling that something was wrong—something physical that I couldn't quite put into words. My joints, once full of energy, began to feel stiff and sore. It was subtle at first, almost like a slow ache creeping up my limbs, but soon, it became more than just an inconvenience. I couldn't shake it.

For six long months, I lived with that persistent discomfort, unsure of what was happening to me. Then, the seizures began. They were terrifying, sudden, and out of the blue. At first, we didn't know what they were. The episodes looked like I was fainting—my body would go limp, and I would lose consciousness, sometimes for a few moments, sometimes longer. My family was understandably alarmed, but doctors didn't have answers. The tests came back clear. Everything seemed fine, even though I was anything but.

At the time, I was already grappling with anxiety, navigating the complex emotions of being a teenager. I was seeing a therapist to help me cope with the challenges of adolescence. When I began fainting, the situation only seemed to spiral. My therapist suggested something that still stings when I think about it; he told my family to ignore me when I "fainted," convinced I was faking it for attention. I don't blame my parents for trusting the "expert" psychologist. After all, he was the one with the fancy title, the professional degrees, and a whole lot of smug confidence that made him sound like he had it all figured out. At the time, my medical tests weren't showing anything that could explain my symptoms, and everything was happening so quickly. My body was changing in ways that didn't make sense, and my parents were grasping at straws, trying to figure out what was going on.

In hindsight, I get it. They were just trying to help me, trying to understand. So, sure, they trusted this "expert"—the guy who looked at me and decided, with zero physical evidence, that I was just "faking it."

Now, I occasionally tease my parents about it, laughing it off like it's some sort of joke. You know, just a bit of light-hearted banter about the fact that their daughter—who was clearly falling apart—was dismissed as someone just having a bad day. But if I'm honest, the person I still have some serious *anger* towards is that psychologist, Dave.

Oh yes, his name was Dave—*I'm sure it still is*—and he was as smug as they come. He sat there on his stereotypical psychologist chair, confident in his "expert" opinion, telling me that the solution was all in my head. The thing is, I don't think he ever actually listened to what I was saying. It wasn't about me seeking attention or "being dramatic." It was for real, and he couldn't see that. What really got me, though, was how he brushed it all off as a mental health issue without ever actually considering that something physical could be going wrong in my body.

I'll never forget the day he told me, in his oh-so-paternalistic way, that we would "work through it together." His plan? He was going to spin me around in his office chair—yes, you read that right—until I "allegedly" passed out. Apparently, this was his *clinical* solution to seeing whether my fainting episodes were real or just me "faking it." As if dizziness was going to somehow solve the mystery of my health. Spoiler alert: it didn't.

6

Well, here I am now, with a real, very diagnosable autoimmune condition and a whole list of faulty body systems. While I can laugh about it now, I can't help but think—*where the hell did Dave get his qualifications from?* Because, as far as I can tell, he wasn't exactly practising evidence-based medicine. I'd love to see how he explains spinning patients around as a valid form of diagnosis. Maybe I'll send him a copy of my medical chart now— complete with a whole lot of autoimmune chaos— and see if he still thinks it's all in my head.

Of course, I probably should deal with the anger I still feel about all of that, but for now, it's staying nicely suppressed, right where I can conveniently ignore it. I might never know where Dave got his credentials, I sure do know where he got it wrong. And that's enough for me.

So, I'd fall to the ground, and when I would regain consciousness, I would find my family standing over me, their faces marked with confusion or, worse, indifference. I was utterly lost in those moments—feeling as if no one understood or believed me. It felt like a cruel form of isolation. I was struggling, not only with the physical symptoms but with the growing sense that I was invisible in my own family's eyes.

Around this time, I saw my first neurologist. I remember him telling me that when I "fainted," all I needed to do was tell myself to open my eyes because it was impossible for someone to stay unconscious for so long. He believed that I had control over it, that my mind could somehow snap me out of the episodes with just a simple command. His explanation sounded logical at the time, and I wanted to believe him. I wanted there to be an answer, even if it was just a small mental trick to overcome this strange affliction.

It wasn't that simple, though. We quickly discovered that it *was* possible to stay unconscious for far longer than he had suggested. Perhaps the professor just wasn't as experienced with cases like mine as we had hoped, or maybe he simply hadn't seen enough to understand the complexity of what I was going through. Either way, the reality was clear: this wasn't something I could will away. It was beyond me, beyond willpower. From that point on, my journey to understanding became more complicated and more urgent.

The turning point came on a seemingly ordinary day. I was walking with my mum along a concrete sidewalk when it happened again. Only this time, it was different. I fell into a full seizure, my body limp as I hit the hard ground, my head smashing against the unforgiving concrete. The pain as I woke was instant, sharp, and overwhelming, but it was also a jarring wake-up call.

That moment changed everything. It was no longer something that could be dismissed. My family couldn't ignore me any longer. I was in real danger, and something needed to be done. The seizure left a mark not just physically, but emotionally too. It was as if I had finally been seen for what I was going through—something real, not imagined, exaggerated, or faked.

From then, the path became clearer. Doctors started to take me seriously, and after further tests, the course of my life was altered. While the journey ahead would be long, challenging, and at times terrifying, that fall on the sidewalk marked the beginning of my fight for answers. It was no longer about pretending I was fine or forcing myself to live in a world where no one understood. It was about accepting that something was wrong and finding the courage to face it, even when the world around me seemed uncertain.

So, let me take you on a quick journey to the second neurologist I ever saw. Now, this guy was no rookie, but let me tell you, even he had a hard time putting the pieces of the puzzle together. And I wasn't exactly the easy jigsaw to solve—no, my puzzle had missing pieces, a couple of edge pieces that just didn't fit, and some others that were upside down.

I had been sent on a whirlwind tour of tests: EEGs, PET scans, MRIs, blood work—the whole shebang. If there were a medical exam Olympics, I'd have earned a gold medal in "Most Tests Taken." With all this data, it was like I was handing them a treasure map, but the "X" was always in the wrong spot. The issues were clearly there, plain as day—like neon signs flashing *something's wrong here*. My neurologist just couldn't piece it all together.

Eventually, after much head scratching and furrowing of brows, he leaned back in his chair, looked me straight in the eye, and said something I'll never forget: *"This is one issue, not a bunch of them like we originally thought. But, unfortunately, I and the medical industry are still developing and do not have the answer for you."* Well, something along those lines. After all, this was around a decade ago.

Now, this was something refreshing. Here was a guy who didn't try to spin a story or convince me that I was imagining things. He just admitted he didn't have all the answers. That kind of accountability, that willingness to say "I don't know," is something I've come to admire. In fact, I think that level of honesty should be normalised in medicine. Imagine a world where doctors, rather than covering up uncertainty, simply admit when they're stumped. Maybe that should be a class in medical school: "How to say 'I don't know' without sounding like you've failed."

Let's face it: no one likes to admit they don't have the answer—especially not a doctor. But here's the thing: that vulnerability actually commands more respect than all the finger-pointing and narrative-spinning in the world. You see, after a while, I started questioning myself. The medical community was great at suggesting it was all in my head until this neurologist was brave enough to admit the truth. When you hear the same thing over and over again, *that* can make you start thinking maybe they're right. I mean, they've got the degrees, right? They're the ones with all the fancy medical lingo, and I'm just sitting here with a headache and a confused expression. That's the classic *victim blaming* in action, my friends. It's like, "Well, your tests are normal, so clearly, you're the one who's broken."

Let's be real: that kind of narrative does more harm than good. It takes you on a road of self-doubt that leads to nowhere. After a while, you start asking yourself, "Am I crazy? Am I just a hypochondriac?" Spoiler alert: no. I was just someone whose puzzle was still missing a piece—and I needed a doctor to be okay with not having it all figured out yet.

So, hats off to that second neurologist. While he didn't have all the answers, he had the right attitude. And in the end, that respect for both himself and me? Well, that's the kind of thing you hold onto.

If anyone ever tells you, "It's all in your head." Consider asking them if they've considered the possibility that your brain might just be *the most complicated organ* in your body.

Of course, after all the tests, I still needed *answers.* And that's why, despite my admiration for his honesty, I didn't stick with this neurologist. I needed someone who could help me make sense of the mess of symptoms I was dealing with. So, I moved on.

Enter my third neurologist—let's call her Dr. "Right Fit." Now, she's been a total game-changer.

We're actually making progress, piecing things together, figuring out what's going on (and yes, there's still some mystery left, but at least we're heading in the right direction). Even as I work with her now, I can't forget what my second neurologist taught me: sometimes, the right thing to say is simply, "I don't have the answer yet."

Beyond the Diagnosis: A Journey Through the Medical System and Society's Expectations

Fast forward over a decade from where I started, and things look very different. I now live with a systemic autoimmune condition, a diagnosis that, after years of uncertainty, became clear. I take immunosuppressants daily and have some semblance of a medical plan in place, but the road to get here has been long and filled with challenges. I've come to terms with my illness in a way, but the journey is not just about managing physical symptoms or keeping track of treatments. It's about navigating the complex and often frustrating world of the medical system—and dealing with the societal perceptions of being someone who is classified as "sick."

When you live with a chronic illness, particularly one that isn't visible on the outside, the medical system often treats you as an enigma—a puzzle to be solved rather than a person to be understood. In the early years, I felt like I was passed from doctor to doctor, each one offering a new theory but no real answers. The process of being diagnosed with something was a journey in itself. It wasn't just a matter of one test or one visit; it was years of medical evaluations, trial and error with medications, and a constant questioning of whether I was imagining my suffering.

Here's the thing about my autoimmune condition: it's *treated* like lupus, but technically, it's not lupus. Why? Because even though I have *all the symptoms* of lupus, and my blood work is practically screaming "autoimmune disorder," there are key lupus blood indicators that are just... *not there.*

Yeah. That one thing. It's like they looked at my results, nodded seriously, and said, "Yup, you definitely have everything else... but not this particular thing, so, nope, not lupus." So, on all my forms, the doctors write "Systemic Autoimmune Disorder - Treated as Lupus." Definitely a mouthful.

It's a bit of a *technicality*—which, in the world of autoimmune disorders, feels like the medical equivalent of someone telling you, "You almost made it to the finish line, but you tripped at the last second. Better luck next time." So, I'm treated for lupus. I get the medications, the monitoring, the whole autoimmune circus. But technically? *Not lupus.* Just a little technicality. I've learned to live with the ambiguity—though I'll admit, it does make for some really fun, confusing doctor visits where they're all like, "So... you're not lupus... but we're treating you like you are..."

The frustrations didn't stop in the doctor's office. Once I had the autoimmune diagnosis, the real battle began: trying to be seen for who I was, not just the sum of my symptoms. There's a certain weight that comes with being classified as "sick." Society, in its well-meaning but often misguided way, assumes that if you don't look sick, then you must be fine. The number of times I've heard "But you look so good!" or "Are you sure you're really that sick?" is endless. People don't understand that just because I don't walk around with a visible sign of my condition, doesn't mean I'm not constantly fighting to feel okay. The well-intentioned comments can be more isolating than anything else, and they often fail to acknowledge the emotional and mental toll that chronic illness takes.

People have said a lot of messed up things to me over the years. "You're just being dramatic," one person once told me after I explained how a flare-up had left me unable to get out of bed. "I wish I could take a day off for every little thing," another person casually remarked when I had to cancel plans due to exhaustion. These comments, whether intentionally hurtful or not, cut deep. They create a world where your pain is invalidated, where you're made to feel like an imposter in your own body. It's one thing to hear these things from people who don't understand, but it's another when they come from those who should know better—like healthcare professionals or even family members and friends. Well, ex-friends now—good riddance.

The worst of it, though, is the assumption that someone with an invisible illness is faking it or exaggerating. I've been told countless times that I should "just push through it" or "exercise more." The suggestion that if I just tried harder, I'd be better is perhaps the most frustrating aspect of living with a chronic condition. It's not about willpower or determination; it's about managing a complex disease with no cure. There's no magic solution or quick fix, and no amount of pushing myself is going to make the pain go away.

The reality is that living with a chronic illness can be incredibly lonely, even when you're surrounded by people. There's a constant mental and emotional load that comes with trying to explain to others what you're going through, and often, you're left feeling misunderstood or dismissed. The medical system, too, can sometimes add to this sense of alienation. I've had doctors who seemed more interested in moving me through their clinic as quickly as possible than actually listening to my experiences. There have been times when I've felt like just another number in a queue—like I didn't matter as a person, just as a case to be treated.

Over the years, I've learned to advocate for myself. I've learned to speak up when something doesn't feel right and to trust my own knowledge of my body. But it hasn't been easy. The emotional toll that comes with constantly having to justify your pain or your limitations can be overwhelming. I found strength in the times when I was able to stand up for myself, but it hasn't come without its own scars. I've had to face the reality that many people, even well-meaning ones, will never fully understand what it's like to live with a condition like mine. And I've had to come to terms with the fact that it's okay if they don't.

What I want people to understand is that being "sick" isn't just about the physical pain or symptoms; it's about the emotional and psychological weight that comes with navigating a world that often doesn't know how to accommodate people like me. It's about the exhaustion of constantly having to prove that you're not faking it.

It's about the isolation that comes when your struggles are minimised or dismissed by a society that only values visible health.

In the end, my story isn't just about my condition or the physical toll it has taken on my body. It's about resilience in the face of a medical system that doesn't always get it right and a society that doesn't always understand. It's about finding the strength to continue, even when others try to define you by your illness. I am not just the label on my diagnosis; I am a person who lives with this condition, and I am more than the sum of my struggles.

The Defensiveness That Came With Being Doubted

There is something profoundly tolling about being told that what you're experiencing is all in your head or that you must be making it up. This feeling cuts deeper than the physical injuries. I remember the times when my pain and symptoms were met with dismissiveness, when doctors would suggest that I was exaggerating or, worse, fabricating my experiences. It made me feel small, like my body was betraying me in ways I couldn't explain, and no one believed me.

While I no longer face this particular doubt from medical professionals—thanks to years of tests showing an endless string of abnormalities and issues—I can't deny the emotional scars it left. Those early years, when I was constantly being told that my suffering was either imaginary or overstated, have shaped me into someone who is incredibly defensive about what I share with doctors today. I don't think people understand how much it hurts to feel invalidated by the very people who are supposed to help you. When in pain, whether physical or emotional, and you're told that it's all in your head, it plants a seed of doubt that can grow and take root. For so long, I wasn't sure if I was imagining everything or if I was simply unable to explain it in a way that made sense to anyone. I'd leave appointments feeling more confused and isolated than when I walked in. The experience of being doubted was worse than any symptom I had because it made me question my own body, my own reality.

Thankfully, those days are behind me now, or at least they're not as frequent. My test results speak for themselves, showing a long history of abnormalities that prove something is very wrong. Despite the confirmation from specialists, however, I've become hyper-aware of how people respond to what I say about my health. I've built a defensive wall that's hard to lower, even when I'm sitting across from a compassionate doctor who genuinely wants to help. Now, when a healthcare provider questions or even hints at questioning my experiences, it triggers a visceral response. It throws me back into that vulnerable place again, where I have to prove that I'm not lying, that my pain is real, and that I am not exaggerating for attention. I'm defensive because I've been burned. My protective instinct kicks in as a reaction to protect me from being dismissed once again.

This defensiveness doesn't come from a place of arrogance; it's a mechanism built over years of being told that I wasn't credible. I've become hyper-vigilant about how my symptoms are discussed. When a doctor suggests a treatment or a course of action, I don't just accept it blindly anymore. I challenge them to explain it thoroughly. I ask more questions and demand more clarity because, unconsciously, I refuse to go back to a place where my suffering wasn't taken seriously.

I know that this has made me seem more confrontational at times. I'm aware of how it might be perceived by medical staff, especially when I challenge their authority or the way they frame my illness. But I can't help it. It's a response I've cultivated after being made to feel invisible for years. It's hard to trust easily when you've been let down repeatedly. I don't think that trust will ever come as easily as it once might have.

This defensiveness isn't just about protecting my dignity—it's about protecting my mental and emotional health, too. I've been through too much to let anyone, even someone in a white coat, make me feel like my experiences don't matter. My body is mine, my pain is real, and my journey is valid.

I've learned that it's okay to stand my ground.

It's okay to question, to push back, and to demand that the people in charge of my care should see me as a whole person—not just a set of symptoms or a medical case. The emotional toll of being doubted has made me stronger in some ways, but it's also made me cautious. It's a reminder of how deeply the medical system can shape your sense of self-worth and how important it is to advocate for yourself—because if I won't stand up for myself, who will?

The Frustrating Journey Before the Diagnosis

Before getting the official diagnosis and realising it was an autoimmune disease, the process was a *nightmare*—not the kind of nightmare you wake up from. More like the kind that just keeps going on and on, day after day. We'd test for affected conditions related to the body systems, but each time, the results came back negative. And that, my friends, was extremely frustrating.

There was something wrong—*so clearly wrong*—but no one could pinpoint what it was. The tests showed a multitude of issues, yes, but they just couldn't connect the dots to explain why all of these things were happening. Every time the doctor would tell me, *"The tests came back negative,"* I felt like I was hitting a wall. And then, as if to add insult to injury, they would sometimes follow it up with a puzzled look and say, *"Oh, well, you wouldn't want to have..."* and then list off conditions they thought might be *too serious* or *too rare* to consider. I'd sit there, feeling utterly deflated because, honestly, I had all the symptoms of something—*something* was clearly wrong—but the labels, the answers, eluded us.

The real kicker was when I'd end up in the emergency department, falling ill once again, trying to explain this endless list of symptoms to the doctors on call. It was like a never-ending inventory of dysfunction. "Well, I've had some blood clots. Also, I spontaneously bleed internally through my skin. I have seizures. Chronic migraines. Tachycardia. Oh, I get pericarditis. My stomach is inflamed, I have acid issues, and the muscles around my lungs and throat are weak, so my oxygen drops and it looks like asthma. Oh, and I also have a bunch of lesions on my brain.

They'd look at me, wide-eyed, completely confused, and ask, *"What's the diagnosis?"*

I'd give my usual response: *"Oh, I don't have one."*

That's when the panic set in for *everyone*—me included. While all these symptoms had piled up, none of the specialists could connect the dots. They didn't, or couldn't, see the whole picture. They didn't see the bigger process happening in my body, how everything was linked, and how it was all part of something much larger that no one had yet been able to name.

It was like they were reading individual chapters of a book but couldn't understand the storyline because they hadn't put the whole book together. And that felt isolating—*no one* was seeing me as a whole person, just a list of disconnected symptoms. They couldn't find the label, so it didn't make sense to them. And trust me, not having a diagnosis for so long can be incredibly frustrating because while you know your body is falling apart, there's no "thing" to point to and say, *"This is why."*

But now? Now, when I walk into a hospital or see a specialist, I don't have to repeat that whole laundry list of symptoms. I don't have to go through the entire saga of *"Well, I have this, and I have that...."* Instead, I can just say, *"I have a systemic autoimmune disease."* And you know what? Everyone knows what's going on. They understand the context. The dots are finally connected. A label doesn't fix everything, but it sure as hell makes things *a lot* easier. It's like finally putting a name to the thing that has been terrorising you for years. It doesn't take away the struggle, but it gives you a framework, a foundation, and, most importantly, a sense of *validation.* It means the process is understood, and that, for me, has made a world of difference.

The Conflicting Comments: "You Don't Look Sick" vs. "You Look Too Sick"

One of the most exhausting parts of living with a chronic illness is the constant barrage of comments about how I look. It's not something you expect, either—those insensitive remarks sometimes come from misunderstanding. It's the contradictions. One moment, people tell me I look *too sick*, the next, they say I don't look sick at all. Both types of comments carry their own weight, but the former has its own peculiar sting.

I've lost count of the number of times I've heard someone say, "You don't look sick." The phrase often depends entirely on how much makeup I wear that day. When I'm well-groomed and wear a full face of makeup, I can almost guarantee that someone will comment on how I look "much better today" or "healthy." But when I don't wear makeup, when the dark circles under my eyes are more prominent, or when my skin colour is off, the tone shifts. It's as if the makeup is some sort of armour that shields me from judgment, but without it, I risk opening myself up to unsolicited opinions about my appearance.

It becomes draining, this constant expectation to maintain a "mask." A full face of makeup feels like a necessity—not just a personal choice, but a social one. Without it, people feel the need to tell me that I don't look well, to highlight the fact that something is wrong with me. It's always the same remarks: "You don't look too well," "Are you okay?" "You look exhausted." It's usually directed at the colouring of my skin or the dark circles around my eyes—things that are inevitable with a chronic condition.

I can't help but wonder: if I know I'm sick and the other person knows that I'm sick, why do they feel the need to inform me of it? It's as if they think I'm unaware of the changes in my body or that I somehow need reminding that I don't look *well.* There's an odd dissonance between what's happening in my body and how my condition is perceived, especially by people who know what I'm going through. Perhaps it's out of concern, but it often comes off as rude and unnecessary. It feels like a comment on my body as a whole, as if my appearance is up for public discussion, despite the fact that I never invited it.

And for those who don't know me, those who don't have the context of my medical condition, the comments feel even worse. It's as if I'm being reduced to nothing more than a reflection in the mirror. To have someone you don't even know point out your physical flaws is uncomfortable at best—and infuriating at worst. In those moments, I never know how to respond.

Am I supposed to say, "I know?" Should I thank them for their concern, or should I just acknowledge their observation? Or perhaps the answer is something much more honest and cathartic: "F**k off."

I often find myself in that middle space, where the proper response feels elusive because no matter how I react, I feel like being judged—either for looking "too sick" or not looking sick enough. It's exhausting to have to navigate these comments while already managing the weight of my condition.

It's ironic, too. I never signed up for this. I didn't ask for anyone's opinion about my appearance. Yet it's a constant part of my life now—these conflicting comments and unsolicited observations, as if my physical appearance is up for debate. If it's not about me looking "too sick," it's about me looking "not sick enough." They leave me feeling uncomfortable, unsure of where I stand in the eyes of others.

The Toughness of Life: Empathy vs. Pity

In many ways, I do have a hard life. I can't deny that. The health challenges, the endless rounds of doctor visits, and the unpredictable flare-ups; they all add up to a life that's far from easy. But so does everyone else's. It's easy to forget that. Their struggle might be different than mine, but the difficulty of life doesn't really have one measure, does it? Who gets to decide what constitutes a "tough" life?

When people hear things like I "suffer" from seizures, they often assume that my life is defined by these conditions—that they must be the sole measure of my experience. And I get it, it sounds heavy. It's hard not to react when you hear something like that. But what about the invisible struggles, the ones that aren't immediately obvious? Anxiety, depression, chronic fatigue, or the mental toll of living with a medical condition that others can't see. These things don't always get the same attention, and they should. They shape my life just as much as my physical symptoms. Yet, these challenges are often dismissed because they aren't as dramatic or "diagnosable" as a brain lesion or seizure.

Yes, in many ways, having multiple medical issues has undeniably created toughness. I've had to learn to adjust and adapt, to find strength in places I never thought I'd have to search. But that's not the issue. It isn't the difficulty of my life or the toll my conditions take on me that bothers me most. It's the way people respond to them. The problem isn't empathy—it's pity.

Empathy is nice. It's the genuine understanding that helps you feel seen and supported. When someone expresses empathy, it feels comforting, like they are walking alongside you, even if they can't truly understand the full weight of what you carry. That kind of response, which doesn't feel condescending, I appreciate.

But what really gets to me is the pity in people's voices. You know the tone—the one that drips with sorrow or disbelief as if to say, "How *can* you live with this? How *could* you possibly have any joy or success in your life with all that's wrong with you?" It's in the way they look at you, as though the mere fact of your illness is a reason to assume your life is somehow diminished, that you are somehow less than what you could have been without it.

I've had people tell me that they're "so sorry" for the way I'm living, making my life a series of tragedies I'm just enduring until the end. It's as if they think my medical condition is the defining feature of who I am, and in turn, it makes them feel sad for me like I'm some tragic figure in a movie. It's almost as if they forget I still have a life beyond the medical chart. Yes, I've had setbacks, and yes, there are days when I'm struggling. But those things don't define me.

The pity, though, suggests that it does. It suggests that my value is diminished because of what I've been through. I can't possibly live a good life because of the conditions that I have. And that's a tough pill to swallow. People assume that having a serious medical condition automatically means I can't find joy, success, or satisfaction in life. But the reality is, I do. I have many moments of joy. I have successes. I've built a life that includes more than just my illness. Every time someone says "I'm so sorry" with that pitying tone, it's as if they're telling me I shouldn't be happy or that I *can't* be happy because my life is inherently tragic.

It's all a bit dramatic, isn't it? To look at someone and immediately conclude that because they have a medical condition, they're somehow bound to a life that's sadder or less meaningful than someone else's. We're all fighting battles in different ways, and none of them should diminish the worth of our lives. We all have something that makes our lives hard, but we also have something that makes our lives worth living.

I've learned to live with my illness, but I've also learned to live *beyond* it. It's just one part of who I am, not the sum of my existence. And I wish more people would see it that way. I don't need your pity. What I need is for you to see me as I am—a person with struggles, yes, but also a person with dreams, joy, and potential. My illness doesn't make me tragic, and it doesn't make my life less valuable. It just makes me different.

The Great "You'll Be Okay" Conspiracy: A Story of False Hope and Mild Annoyance

At first, I didn't think much of it. Someone would hear about my symptoms, pause dramatically, tilt their head like a concerned golden retriever, and then say it. *"You'll be okay."*

A simple phrase. Harmless, really. Or so I thought.

As you know, I was a relatively normal 15-year-old going about my business, and the next day, I was a full-time medical mystery. I started noticing some *quirks*—like my joints randomly deciding they didn't feel like participating in daily activities. They'd just sort of... *lock up*. Now, I'm fully aware that "locking up" is *not* an official medical term, but 15-year-old me was feeling descriptive, and honestly, it captured the experience perfectly. So, we rolled with it.

Naturally, I started mentioning this to people. You know, as you do when your body suddenly starts behaving like a rusty old tin man. And people reacted as expected: with a mix of mild confusion and that ever-so-classic, *"Huh, that's weird."* Yes, Brenda, it *is* weird. I'm so glad we had this enlightening conversation.

Then came the next level of fun: seizures. And, for added excitement, my heart decided to race constantly for no apparent reason, as if it were personally training for the Olympics. And that's when I noticed something truly bizarre—not from my body this time, but from the people around me.

The great "You'll Be Okay" movement had begun.

At first, I thought it was just a one-off thing. Someone would hear about my symptoms, do a little concerned head tilt, and then say it. *"You'll be okay."* A simple phrase. Harmless, really. But then... it kept happening. Over and over. Like some kind of scripted response, people were programmed to say when confronted with *mild-to-moderate* medical horror stories.

I started to wonder: was this for *me* or *them*? Because let's be real—how did they know? Were they secretly consulting with my doctors? Had they obtained a leaked copy of my medical records? Were they *clairvoyant*? No, of course not. They were just winging it with 100% unfounded confidence.

And let me tell you, their delivery was not

reassuring. It was more of a *frantic reassurance*—like a desperate attempt to manifest a good outcome purely by saying the words out loud. I could practically see them sweating.

Karen (because, let's face it, there's always a Karen) would take a deep breath, clutch her metaphorical pearls, and go, *"You'll be okay."* And I would stand there, blinking at her, thinking, *Are you telling me, or are you telling yourself, Karen?* If you're trying to manifest a better situation for me, at least throw in some jazz hands or a dramatic spell-casting gesture. Make it believable.

The best part? I was apparently supposed to just *accept* this declaration like it had magical healing properties. As if Karen had spoken my fate into existence, and now, thanks to her profound wisdom, all my medical issues would disappear. Phew! That was a close one. Thank goodness Karen showed up just in time to rewrite the laws of science and medicine!

Of course, reality had other plans. Things do *not* miraculously get better just because people said they would. In fact, they got significantly worse. By all physical metrics, my body was on a downward spiral, completely unfazed by the verbal placebo effect people were trying to push on me.

But in the end, I *am* okay. More than okay. Just... not because of Karen's unwavering faith in the power of empty words.

So, thanks, I guess? I mean, without all those helpful proclamations of my inevitable wellness, who knows where I'd be today? I might have just given up, not realising that the simple phrase *"You'll be okay"* was the key to eternal health and happiness.

Moral of the story: it's okay not to know what to say. You don't have to fill the silence with baseless optimism. A simple *"Dang, that must be scary"* would have sufficed. Heck, I'd have even accepted a *"Wow, that sucks"*—at least it would've been honest. But no, we went with mass delusion instead.

And that, dear reader, is how I became a skeptic of unsolicited reassurance.

See, I genuinely don't think people meant any harm. I think they truly believed they were being helpful, reassuring, and supportive. And that's what brings me to my next point: people do not know how to validate.

Like, at all.

Somewhere along the way, we collectively decided that validation means telling someone everything will be fine. But that's not what validation is. Validation is saying, *"I can only imagine how tough this must be."* It's *"That sounds really scary."* It's *"That seriously sucks, and I'm here for you."* It's acknowledging what someone is going through rather than trying to talk them out of their feelings.

And I can only imagine the sheer number of friends, family, coworkers, and well-meaning acquaintances who *think* they are validating when, in fact, they are not.

And just to be clear—this is not some kind of *"You're not doing good enough"* saga. This is not a dramatic call-out post for everyone who's ever fumbled through a supportive conversation. This is simply for awareness. Because, in reality, *you don't need to fill the gaps.* You don't need to magically fix the situation with empty words. It's okay to just say, *"Dang, that must be really hard."*

Trust me, it'll go a lot further than a half-panicked, wildly inaccurate "You'll be okay."

The Relationship Question: "But How Will You Ever Find a Partner?"

Ah, the eternal question: "But how will you ever find a partner?" *Cue the dramatic gasp* as if the mere thought of someone wanting to be with someone who is "sick" is utterly unfathomable. It's almost as if people think that the second you get a diagnosis, you become a relationship pariah, destined to live alone forever. Apparently, having a chronic illness is like wearing a sign that says, "Do not touch—bad luck." Who knew?

Let's get one thing straight: I've been married—*once*—and, spoiler alert, I'm sure I'll be married again. And guess what? My autoimmune condition was never a dealbreaker. I mean, sure, my ex-husband and I had a few other issues—don't we all?—but my health didn't make the top 10 list of things we disagreed on. It wasn't like we were sitting there during the wedding vows, and I was like, "I do, but just so you know, I come with a side of unpredictable flare-ups and a whole bunch of medical appointments." Instead, we just lived, as people do—together, with the usual baggage, the usual quirks, and, yes, the occasional tantrum about my body doing its own thing. But the autoimmune stuff? Not the issue.

Now that I'm single again, people seem to love to remind me that it's "going to be hard to find a partner" because of my health. Apparently, no one could possibly love someone who sometimes requires naps in the middle of the day or who might collapse into a heap on the floor because their body decided to throw a tantrum. It's as if chronic illness is a relationship killer and I've just missed the memo.

When I was married, people loved to call my ex-husband an "angel." And no, it wasn't because he had the patience of a saint when dealing with my *unquestionably delightful* attitude. (I know, shocker.) It wasn't because he had the grace of a swan when I had a flare-up or needed help getting to yet another doctor's appointment. No, it was because he was somehow able to "put up" with my illness. It was as though he'd been cast in the role of the long-suffering partner who bravely dealt with the emotional and physical burden of someone who wasn't in perfect health. *Angel*—I'm not sure about that, but he was certainly good at getting me a heat pack when my tummy hurt.

But here's the thing: *everyone* comes into relationships with their fair share of baggage. I mean, come on, do we really think anyone gets through life without a few scars, quirks, or strange habits? My medical condition was just one of many things we navigated, and it wasn't any harder than the usual stuff people deal with—like whether or not to leave the toilet seat up or how to split Netflix time. And honestly, none of my "baggage" really had anything to do with my health. But apparently, in the eyes of some people, having a chronic condition is the one thing that makes a relationship truly *impossible.*

So, to answer the question: I'll be fine. I've got more than enough love and humour in my life to keep things interesting. And I'll find a partner when the time's right, autoimmune condition or not. I'm not looking for someone to "save" me; I'm not some tragic figure who needs pity or an angel on a pedestal. And if someone can't handle a little autoimmune chaos mixed into a relationship, well, I suppose that's their loss. There are *plenty* of people out there who can appreciate a strong, witty person with a full life, whether it includes autoimmune flares or not.

And for those who keep asking, "But how will you ever find a partner?"—well, I'll just give them a wink and say, "Don't worry. I've got it covered. And in the meantime, I'm *loving* my own company."

As you now know, when people assume that anyone who wants to be with me must be a *saint* because they have to deal with my chronic illness, it really gets me frustrated. It's not just the words that sting; it's the underlying assumption that my health issues define me—and, by extension, that my partner's entire role in the relationship is to be some kind of long-suffering hero who's *taking on the burden* of my illness.

Let me just clear something up: I am more than my autoimmune condition. It doesn't make up my entire existence, even if some people seem to think it does. And while I appreciate the suggestion that my future partner might need divine patience, I can assure you, I'm not some tragic figure who's forever defined by the fact that my body occasionally decides to throw a temper tantrum. I'm still *me*—complicated, flawed, and definitely not some tragic, illness-ridden stereotype that needs saving.

Maybe my career in social work has given me an ear for anti-oppressive language, but what's really concerning isn't just that people vocalise these thoughts. It's that they genuinely believe them. They actually think that the act of having a chronic illness makes me somehow less capable of living a full, happy life—and that anyone who loves me must be some sort of martyr for doing so. There's a weird and misguided sense that chronic illness is this all-consuming identity, one that overshadows everything else I am. And that's not just flawed—it's oppressive.

It's almost like people see my medical chart, make a snap judgment, and say, "Okay, so she's got *this* condition, and therefore that must be her entire personality." Like, surprise—my illness isn't my identity. I'm still the person I've always been despite needing a little extra care sometimes. That doesn't make me some tragic, saint-in-waiting who can only find love if someone is willing to "sacrifice" for me.

And here's the thing: the idea that someone has to be an angel for wanting to be with me? That's insulting. Not just to me, but to the idea of partnership in general. Relationships, at their core, are about mutual support, respect, and understanding—not about one person heroically carrying the weight of the other's health issues. My chronic illness doesn't make me a burden, and it doesn't make my partner a saint. It just makes me someone who needs to take care of myself and sometimes asks for help—like most people do, whether they have a medical condition or not.

So, when people say things like, "Oh, your partner must be a saint," it doesn't just brush over the fact that I'm *also* bringing something to the table—it reduces my entire experience to something to be pitied. It's not a relationship if one person is just *serving* the other. It's a partnership. And I'm not looking for someone to "deal" with me. I'm looking for someone who's ready to face the ups and downs with me, not as a caretaker or a martyr, but as an equal.

I'll tell you this: if someone is willing to be with me just because they think they're doing me a favour, then I'm *really* not interested. But if someone can see me as a whole person—with my quirks, laughter, dreams, and yes, even my health challenges—then we'll get along just fine. Because at the end of the day, love doesn't come with conditions like, "Do you have a medical condition? No? Okay, great, you're in." It comes with the understanding that we all have our baggage, our flaws, and our struggles. My health is just one part of that. And it definitely doesn't define me, no matter how many people want to act like it does.

My Health History Isn't Your Baggage–But Thanks for the Concern

Now, I'm a firm believer that your medical history should never become your personal baggage, but let's talk about this for a second because some people seem to forget that this is, in fact, my journey, not theirs. It's something I deal with, not something I'm asking them to carry. My health is just part of the story. It's *my* story, and it's not a burden to anyone else unless they make it one.

So here's the deal: so far, I've been lucky. I've never had someone I was dating throw up their hands and say, *"Whoa, this is way too much for me, I'm out."* But, as I just got back into the dating pool, in the wonderful world of dating, I do dread the classic "so, do you want kids?" question that just *has* to come up. And, let me tell you, I'm already feeling the nerves. See, technically, I *can* have children, but it's not exactly a walk in the park for my body. We're talking about signing up for an intense boot camp my body didn't exactly ask for. The doctors haven't told me "no," but they've definitely voiced their concerns about what it could do to my body, especially in its current state. When I mentioned that maybe it's best not to carry children myself, their reaction was honestly... relieved.

But hey, that's where things stand right now, and I'm in a better place than I was, stabilising more and more with meds. Who knows, I might change my mind when I'm feeling better! There are also other options like surrogacy, so it's not like the door is totally closed. It's just that, you know, having this kind of conversation isn't exactly something you're going to bring up on the first date—or even the second.

It's a huge topic, and I'm not about to dive into it until I'm already in love (because nothing says "romantic" like talking about reproduction, right?). And while I'm sure it'll lead to some tricky and possibly awkward conversations, I'm confident that for the right person, it won't be a problem. If they're the one, we'll figure it out together. So, I guess I'm just going to brace myself for the awkward questions and trust that the right person will understand and be there through it all. So I'm sure someone along the way will throw up their hands and say, *"Whoa, this is way too much for me, I'm out."* If that happens, fine—respect.

Everyone's got their own dealbreakers, their own limits. I don't expect everyone to be on board with every chapter of my life. But here's the thing: I'm not looking for sympathy, and my medical history is not an issue unless you make it one. So, if someone's going to walk away from a potential connection because of my health, cool, that's their prerogative. But just know this: it's not a reflection of *me,* it's a reflection of their preferences. And hey, *each to their own*, right?

Funnily enough, most people making comments about my health—about how it could be too much or how they just *couldn't handle it*—aren't the ones actually dating me. Isn't that convenient? It's like people on the sidelines who have a lot to say about how the game should be played, but none are on the field. So, to all those well-meaning but over-involved "concerned citizens" in my life (looking at you, Karen), maybe it's time to take a step back. You're not the one who has to share my bed or my time, so your opinion on how much "baggage" I have isn't exactly solicited.

Honestly, if my health is too much for someone, I can live with that. I'm not for everyone, and that's fine. But let's be real: maybe Karen's inability to stay out of my business is *more* of a problem for her partner than my health is for me. Just putting that out there. At least when it comes to my health, I'm not trying to project it onto anyone else or make them carry it for me. But some people can't resist the urge to weigh in on things they have zero business in. So, maybe *that* is the real baggage to worry about.

To anyone ever worried about whether my health is an issue, here's the deal: it's mine. If you're in the dating pool and my history doesn't scare you, great. If it does, that's okay too. But let's be clear: it's not *your* baggage to carry. And if you're not dating me, maybe keep the commentary to yourself. Your relationship drama is probably more baggage than my health history could ever be.

The "You Should Do This" Diet Parade

You know what's *really* fun? When people seem to have *the answer* for how to cure me. Everyone has the magic formula to heal my autoimmune condition. It's always a story about someone who had exactly the same condition—*except it's never the same as mine*—and now they're living their best life, never getting sick, doing yoga on mountaintops, and drinking green juice. Oh, if only it were that easy.

And here's the real kicker: the advice always contradicts itself. One person will swear up and down that an all-vegan diet—no meat, no dairy—is the secret to *healing* my body. The very same day, someone else will tell me I need to follow a Mediterranean diet packed with meat and fish. I can't even keep up with the contradictions. I mean, should I be gnawing on carrots and quinoa or roasting lamb with olive oil? Maybe a little of both? Who knows.

I've tried a fair share of these diets, and let's be real, they start off as the *"new me!"* but quickly turn into a massive pain in the ass. The worst one? A zero-sugar diet. You know, the kind that tells you to cut out fructose, too, which, surprise, includes all the delicious fruits I love. Oh, how tragic! Goodbye, sweet, juicy mangoes and berries. I'm now staring at a plate of kale, wishing to have a banana to go with it. Can we take a moment for that loss?

Here's the thing: *short-term,* these diets sound manageable, even... simple. But long-term, especially in an Italian family? Forget it. When Nonna's making homemade pasta and *sugo*, you don't exactly throw a fit and say, "Sorry, Nonna, I can't eat your cooking because I'm on the latest cleanse." That's a one-way ticket to being *disowned* by the whole family. And even if you *do* manage to avoid it for a little while, you're still getting sick, and you're still flaring up. So, I decided: if I'm going to flare up, I might as well do it with some damn good food. The *treats* aren't going anywhere, and honestly, neither am I.

Now, don't get me wrong—my diet still gets impacted by my condition. The meds I'm on have this lovely side effect of making me nauseous all the time, so I end up eating small meals frequently just to avoid spending half my day with my head in the toilet. It's fun. But I do try to keep it reasonably clean. I mean, I'm not out here surviving on potato chips and chocolate (though, honestly, that would be *delightful*). But the truth is, a little treat here and there never killed anyone, and sometimes a cupcake is just the thing to make your day feel *normal*.

Oh, don't get me wrong—I'm not out here calling every single person who's ever talked to me about diet a total menace. That's not the case at all. In fact, I once had a family member who practically made it his part-time job. He knew my symptoms quite well, could probably recite my blood work like a dramatic monologue, and actually worked *with* doctors to find some natural options—not to replace my medication, but to *support* it. And no, I'm not saying I expect that level of dedication from everyone—I'm not out here handing out homework assignments. But there's a big difference between someone who actually knows me and wants to help... and someone who's just confidently talking out of their a**, armed with nothing but a hunch and a YouTube video they half-watched once. That's the difference, right? There's a world of difference between someone who genuinely cares and does their homework... and some random person at the grocery store who takes one look at me and decides I *desperately* need to hear their TED Talk on kale.

So, to all the people who love offering diet advice, here's my challenge: you go first. Follow your diet plan for a week, see how you feel, and then come talk to me. Until then, I think I'll stick with what works for my body—and that includes a slice of pizza every now and then. And hey, if it makes me sick, at least I can say I went down with a delicious *flame* of carbs and cheese.

A Little Perspective on Health and Dieting

Here's a thought to chew on: have you ever walked up to someone and said, *"You need to go on a diet?"* No? Well, I hope not because for a lot of people, that would be considered pretty rude. So why is it that when someone has a health condition, suddenly, it's okay to offer unsolicited advice? It's not. It's really not.

Now, I get it. People want to help, and they think that offering diet tips or "solutions" is just the thing. Here's the truth: *dieting is hard*—for everyone. Just because I have a health condition doesn't somehow make it easier for me to diet. In fact, it can be even more challenging, considering that sometimes what works for one person doesn't work for another. Just because I'm dealing with a chronic issue doesn't mean I'm suddenly an expert at navigating what I can and can't eat.

But here's the twist: I *am* receptive to conversations about food and dieting. I follow a FODMAP diet, and for me, it's been a game-changer. I find the science behind it fascinating, and it genuinely helps my stomach when it's flaring up. I could talk about all the different diets out there for hours if you want to dive into the details. But—and this is important—*don't start by telling me what to do.*

Dieting isn't a one-size-fits-all solution, and neither is managing a chronic condition. I've done the research. I've tried things. I'm open to suggestions from experts or thoughtful people, but *please* don't make it about what you think I should be doing. Offer support, not unsolicited advice. Trust me, when it comes to health, we're all doing the best we can. Just like you wouldn't tell someone on the street to go on a diet, let's also consider that a health condition doesn't make it any easier for someone to navigate food and wellness.

So let's keep it simple: be kind, be mindful, and save the "helpful tips" for when they're actually asked for.

Exercise: The Never-Ending Suggestions

Let's talk about *exercise*, shall we? Apparently, everyone has the perfect solution for me when it comes to *moving my body*. You name it—exercise, ice baths, time in the sun, stretching, yoga, you name it. Everyone's got an opinion about what will cure me, and the advice keeps coming, even though I've got a *65-hour work week* to get through before I can even consider *sunbaking* my way to health. Oh, sure, Mother Nature has all the answers. Right. Let me just clock out of work, jump into an ice bath, and soak up some sun before going back to managing a full-time job, chronic illness, and my social life. No big deal.

But exercise? Oh boy, let's dive into that one. Over the last year, I've been doing *quite well* with exercise—*for me*. But don't get it twisted; it hasn't always been that way. For a long time, I wanted *nothing* to do with it. Exercise? No thanks. It wasn't just about laziness. It was about my joints. You know that feeling when you exercise and your muscles are sore the next day? Yeah, imagine that, but with your joints. And instead of a little soreness, you can't walk the next day. Or climb stairs. Or, well, move. So, no, I wasn't really signing up for a 5K anytime soon.

Then, on top of that, let's talk about *fatigue*. Oh, the fatigue. It's not like the kind of tiredness where you just need a nap. It's like your entire body is dragging you down, and the thought of moving even a little is an insurmountable mountain. I'm talking about the kind of fatigue that makes getting off the couch feel like trying to summit Everest. It's not about getting up to do a triathlon. Hell, some days, it's just about walking around the block. That's it. I'd give it my best shot, and the next thing I knew, I was flat on my back, a heat pack on my joints, tears rolling down my face, and popping painkillers like they were candy. Doesn't sound too "healthy," huh?

Then, of course, my autoimmune decided to have a little fun and target my lungs because why not add *that* to the mix? Suddenly, I had to manage dropping oxygen levels. So now I've got to stay *super* aware of my body, knowing the exact moment to sit my a** down and *breathe*. Turns out, your body can get pretty good at functioning on low oxygen, which means you might not even realise how badly you're doing until things get serious. I wasn't exactly planning on becoming an expert in oxygen levels.

Who knew this came with the autoimmune territory?

And lLet me tell you something. Every time someone—well-meaning or not—gets *all up in my grill* about how "exercise is *so* good for me," I just have one thing to say: I have definitely visualised punching you in the face. And you know what? It felt good. Just a quick mental fantasy of letting my fist do the talking because, somehow, *I'm the one who knows my body.* I don't need your unsolicited advice, thanks.

Alright, I probably shouldn't even waste my breath on this, but here I am, about to give my two cents anyway. Lately, there's been a lot of chatter about my exercise regime, as if I'm out here doing weekly spin classes and somehow that's the magic fix to all my problems. The truth is, exercise is a wonderful tool for health—don't get me wrong, I'm not against it. It promotes circulation, keeps your heart healthy, and has some serious mental health benefits too. But here's the thing: exercise doesn't cure autoimmune diseases.

And honestly, if you're the one making all these comments about how much I should or shouldn't be working out, can we just take a second to ask: *Why aren't you exercising yourself?* Maybe, just maybe, it's not a simple "lack of motivation" situation. Maybe there's a reason why people aren't hitting the gym or going for that morning run. I'm sure you already know that, right? It's not like everyone's out here skipping their spin class for fun.

Look, I get it; exercise is a good thing for *everyone.* But, just for the record, my knees don't exactly feel like they're made of rubber. I've had them dislocated six times, and the swelling in my joints is a daily reminder that, yeah, my body is a bit of a *special project.* So, here's the deal: if you want to talk to me about exercise, that's cool. We can chat about it. But unless you've walked (or, let's be honest, limped) in my shoes—or better yet, walked with my knees—you probably don't have the full picture.

I don't want to sound cliche, but until you've had a knee that's popped out of place six times or felt the kind of joint swelling that makes even rolling over in bed feel like a chore, maybe, just maybe, keep your "helpful" suggestions to yourself. I mean, I'm all for advice, but let's not pretend that your quick fix is a one-size-fits-all solution when you're not the one living with the reality of a body that's a little *extra* in all the wrong ways.

So yeah, exercise is great. It's *important.* But it's not the magic pill for autoimmune disease, and it's definitely not the only thing to consider when someone's dealing with chronic pain or a compromised body. And while we're at it, let's stop assuming we know everyone else's story. Maybe there's more going on behind the scenes than a missed spin class or skipped yoga session. Just a thought.

And when you've spent a few years trying to *not* move just so you can *move* tomorrow, let me know how your workout routine is going. Until then, I'll continue to take it one step at a time—literally—and on my own terms.

Meet My Uninvited Roommates

Once upon a time, in a land where careers made sense, I was a therapist. I studied social work, but instead of diving into the bureaucratic jungle of paperwork and policies, I chose the path of one-on-one therapy. It was fascinating, rewarding, and occasionally involved nodding empathetically while someone explained their deep emotional attachment to their childhood pet rock. I genuinely loved it. I became one of *those* people—the kind who actually enjoys reading about new therapy modalities in their free time.

Of course, life had other plans. Why settle for one stable career when you can throw yourself into a complete professional 180? Despite my career switch, I never fully left the therapy world. These days, I get my fix as a lecturer and tutor in counselling, which means I get paid to stand in front of a room full of students, wave my hands dramatically, and say things like, "Let's talk about emotional resilience!" I still adore therapy—just from a slightly safer distance, where my clients are mostly stressed-out students who regret leaving their assignments until the last minute.

One of my favourite counselling approaches is *narrative therapy*, which is all about externalising problems. Essentially, it helps people see that *they are not their issues*—which is incredibly useful when dealing with things like anxiety, self-doubt, or, in my case, a body that occasionally behaves like a rebellious teenager. So, naturally, I took this concept and ran with it. I didn't just externalise problems in the metaphorical sense—I started *naming them*.

What started as a small personal quirk has now spiralled into a full-blown tradition. My friends, my family, my doctors—everyone is in on it. When you have chronic health issues, giving them ridiculous names makes them slightly less infuriating. And, let's be honest, much easier to curse at.

Bloody Albert

The first, and perhaps most infamous, of my uninvited roommates is *Albert*. Bloody Albert. Now, Albert *technically* has a fancy medical name, something to do with cell populations and inflammation and blah blah blah—whatever, science. But all you need to know is that Albert lives right at the bottom of my sternum (I *think* I'm getting the anatomy right) and causes a highly localised, golf-ball-sized area of searing pain. He's like a tiny, invisible demon with a fondness for surprise attacks.

Whenever Albert flares up, instead of saying, "I'm in pain" or "I feel awful," I simply groan, "Bloody Albert." And, like magic, my friends and family immediately understand. No long-winded explanation is needed. Albert has become so notorious that even my doctor has started referring to him by name. "How's Albert doing?" they'll ask as if he's a grumpy old neighbour rather than a pain problem. And honestly? That's *way* less depressing than the alternative.

Stacy, the Steroid Sorceress of Doom

Then there's *Stacy*. Stacy isn't a physical condition—oh no, she's something far more insidious. Stacy is a full-blown *alter ego*.

Anyone who has ever been on high doses of steroids (or had their doses adjusted) knows that these medications have a special talent for turning even the most rational, easygoing person into an emotional *volcano*. One minute, you're fine. The next, you're crying because someone ate the last slice of pizza, and then you're inexplicably *furious* about something you definitely wouldn't care about in normal circumstances. It's like PMS on steroids. (*Literally.*)

The tricky thing is, when you're *in* the moment, you don't *feel* irrational. You feel *justifiably outraged.* You're convinced that, no, this time, you're *actually* mad. It's only *after* the emotional storm has passed that you realise—oh. *Oops.* That wasn't me. That was *Stacy.*

Now, to be clear, Stacy is not an excuse. She's not some scapegoat I use to avoid accountability. Trust me, my family has *zero* problem humbling me when necessary. But it *does* help to acknowledge that sometimes, my reactions under steroid influence are... well, *not great.* So, instead of wallowing in embarrassment after an unnecessary meltdown, I just take a deep breath and say, "Okay. That was Stacy. My bad.

Terry, the Tumour

Just when I thought I had enough honorary roommates, along came *Terry.* Terry, the Tumour.

Sounds ominous, right? But before you panic, let me assure you—Terry is *friendly.* Not the scary, evil, life-threatening kind of tumour. He's just a benign little blob, hanging out in a completely non-dangerous part of my brain, living his best life rent-free. Every year, my neurologist checks in on him, measures his size, and gives me the green light to ignore him for another twelve months.

But let's be real—if a doctor tells you, "You have a *tumour* in your brain," your immediate reaction is *not* going to be, "Oh, cool, no big deal." It's going to be sheer, unfiltered panic. Because the word *tumour* is scary. It has Big Bad Energy. It doesn't matter if the doctor reassures you that it's totally harmless— you hear "tumour," and your brain starts planning a dramatic farewell speech.

So I did what I do best—I externalised. I named him Terry. And suddenly, it wasn't, *Oh my God, I have a brain tumour.* It was, *Ugh, Terry is such a freeloader.* See? *Way* less terrifying.

At this point, you might be wondering: *Why do you do this?* Why assign cute, slightly ridiculous names to conditions that, frankly, suck?

Because, dear friends, life is *hard enough.* When your body throws curveballs at you on a regular basis, sometimes the best way to cope is to turn those curveballs into characters. It's not about ignoring reality—it's about making reality slightly more manageable. It's about shifting the narrative from *this is scary and overwhelming* to *ugh, Albert is being a pain again*.

It also helps the people around me understand what's going on without me having to explain my entire medical history every five minutes. If I say, "Albert's acting up," my friends know I need to sit down. If I say, "Stacy made an appearance today," my family knows to tread lightly. And if I mention that Terry's still hanging out, my neurologist knows I'm keeping my sense of humour intact.

So, if you, too, have a chronic health condition, might I suggest giving it a name? It won't make the symptoms go away, but at least you'll have something fun to yell at when things get frustrating. And trust me—there's something oddly satisfying about shaking your fist at the sky and yelling, *Damn you, Albert!*

So, if you're someone grappling with the *new and exciting* list of issues that come with autoimmune life—congratulations! You've just unlocked a thrilling adventure filled with mysterious symptoms, surprise doctor visits, and an ever-growing collection of prescription bottles. Feeling overwhelmed? That's completely normal. But might I suggest a strategy?

Give the weird a wonderful *name*. Your unpredictable joint pain? Maybe that's *Greg*, who only shows up when you have important plans. That relentless brain fog? *Susan*, who makes sure you forget why you walked into a room. That one symptom your doctor can't explain but insists is "probably fine?" *Kevin*, the enigma.

Naming things won't fix them. But it *will* give you something to curse at when your body decides to throw a tantrum. And honestly? That little bit of humour makes all the difference. Because if you have to deal with Albert, Stacy, and Terry showing up uninvited—you might as well make them earn their place in the story.

Now, if you'll excuse me, I need to go argue with Stacy about why it's *really* not appropriate to cry over the last slice of cake.

The "What Do You Do?" Question and the "You Can Do *That?*" Response

Ah yes, the age-old question: *"What do you do?"*

For someone who works a *65-hour week* (sometimes more, because why not, right?), this question pops up a lot. People are genuinely curious—though I have my suspicions that it's more about them trying to figure out how the hell I manage all that with, you know, my autoimmune condition. Spoiler alert: *I get it done.* But for now, let's focus on the real question that follows: *"What did you study at university?"*

Oh, this is where things get interesting. Buckle up.

I've got a *bachelor's degree in Social Work* and a *master's in Peace and Conflict Studies.* Right now, I'm in the process of developing my research area for a PhD. Yeah, I like to keep myself ridiculously busy because why not add a PhD into the mix when you're already juggling a million things? We won't discuss the *why* because we just don't have enough time for that level of introspection, but it's fair to say that I thrive on being productive.

But, here's the thing. When people hear about this little collection of degrees and academic pursuits, the reaction is often... *interesting*. You know, the stock sets in. Some people stare at me like I've grown a second head and say, "I didn't think you would have even finished high school." Well, that's nice, thanks. But it gets better. Some will follow up with, "Wow, isn't that too much for you with, you know, your autoimmune?"

Ummm... Anything you can do, I can do, sick.

When I hear these comments, it honestly makes me laugh. I get it. I *do* have tough days, for sure. My body got its *quirks*, as we've discussed. But guess what? My workplaces have been incredibly accommodating. I've learned a lot about pacing myself, taking breaks, and working around my limitations. Not to forget, I've been dealing with body systems rebelling against me since I was a teenager. You don't go through that without picking up a few tricks along the way.

For example? The *art of sitting in a meeting while in pain* and somehow keeping a straight face. I mean, that's a skill that definitely merits a place on my CV. I should probably add it under "Special Skills"—*ability to nod thoughtfully while internally wishing for death due to joint pain*. If that doesn't scream *professional*, I don't know what does.

But seriously, people just assume that because I have a chronic illness, that means I'm incapable of handling a full workload or pursuing higher education. They think that just because my body sometimes throws a tantrum, I must be out of the game entirely. And sure, some days, my body *wins* the battle. But on the days I'm *fighting back*, I'm getting shit done.

If you were one of those who were shocked specifically about me completing university, there's something I'm a little confused about. Going to university didn't exactly take a massive physical toll on my body to the point where people should be gasping in shock. Like, if I told someone I'd spent all day working under the sun, lifting heavy things, and doing some intense physical labour, sure, I get the shock factor. But sitting in my office, reading literature, and writing essays? That didn't exactly send my autoimmune system into a tailspin. In fact, it was more likely to put my brain on overload than my body.! You'd think I was running a marathon just by writing a research paper. But nope, just the usual university stress. Honestly, it's kind of funny how something as *mentally* exhausting as that can somehow get more of a reaction than actual physical labour.

I guess my question is: what exactly about university did you think I was incapable of handling? Because, let's be real, there's no physical labour involved in reading, writing, and sitting in lectures. Was it the fact that I was there while feeling sick? If that's what threw you off, let me share something a psychologist once told me that completely changed my mindset.

She asked me, "Do you feel sick when you go out?"

I said, "Yeah, sometimes. That's why I stay home when I'm feeling really bad."

She paused for a second, then asked, "Do you feel sick when you're at home?" and

I said, "Yeah, pretty much. It doesn't really change whether I'm out or in."

She looked at me and said, "Well, then go live your life. You may as well be doing the things you love if you're going to be in pain anyways."

That conversation really stuck with me. It made me realise that if I'm going to feel lousy no matter what, I might as well be out there doing what brings me joy, experiencing life and not letting the pain hold me back. It's like, why waste time staying home when you could be living, even if it means you're a little sick while doing it? So, if that's what you were shocked by—seeing me out there despite not feeling great—I guess I'm just living by that advice. Pain doesn't stop me from doing what matters to me.

So, to all the doubters and the ones who think my health defines me? I'm out here, thriving in my own way. Just because I might be sick doesn't mean I'm not capable. And trust me, when I finish my next accomplishment, you'll be asking me, "So, how did you do it?" And I'll be here, smiling and saying, "I learned the hard way, and I didn't stop."

Here's a reflective question for you, especially for the people who like to question my ability to work once they find out about my health conditions: so, you know what I do for work, right? You know the capacity in which I work, the effort I put in, the tasks I handle. We're talking about the day-to-day effort, the deadlines, the emails, the meetings. You see me functioning, doing my thing, right? Now, imagine if you *never* knew about my autoimmune condition. What if I never shared it with you? Would you even think to question my ability to perform at work? Probably not.

Here's the millionth kicker: once you find out about my health conditions—months, maybe even years later—suddenly, you start wondering if I'm really capable of doing what I do. It's almost like the moment you learn about my illness, you start to see me through a different lens, as if that defines my professional abilities or somehow makes me less competent. But why? Why does my health have to suddenly take centre stage when it never even crossed your mind before? If my condition didn't change the way I worked yesterday, why would it change the way I work today?

It's frustrating, right? Because nothing about how I perform at work has changed. Sure, I have to manage my health, and I take that seriously, but *that* doesn't mean I'm not capable of meeting my professional commitments. If anything, my ability to balance health and work is a testament to my time management, resilience, and determination. The only thing that's different is that now you know about my condition—and maybe, just maybe, you're letting that knowledge cloud your judgment about my ability to do my job.

Next time you find yourself questioning someone's ability to perform based on their health, ask yourself: *Would I be questioning this if I didn't know anything about their condition?* If the answer is no, then maybe it's time to stop assuming that someone's health condition defines their professional worth.

From Seizures to Overachieving: A High School Flashback

Honestly, comments like these so far don't really faze me anymore. If anything, they just make me dig my heels in harder. It's like the universe gave me a personal challenge: "Oh, you don't think I can do this? Watch me." So, I guess it's not surprising that I'm now a proud *overachiever*. It's probably part of the reason I'm working 65-hour weeks and keeping up with academic pursuits—I'm just out here trying to prove a point. But I guess this need to constantly *push harder* goes way back. In fact, I've been hearing this kind of talk since I was in high school.

Let's rewind a bit to Year 12, my HSC year. During that time, I was having up to three seizures a day and, on average, around eight per week. It was a lot. I was battling my own body, trying to stay on top of schoolwork, and dealing with the usual teenage angst. But here's the kicker—the new principal (who I'm sure was fresh out of some *very promising* leadership course) decided to pull my mum and me into a meeting with the school counsellor. They slid a list of my absences across the table like it was some kind of trophy—"Look how many times she's missed class!" They then proceeded to go on and on about how my struggles were going to negatively impact my future. They suggested that I do my HSC over *two years* instead of one because, clearly, there was no way I could handle the workload with all the classes I had missed. And to top it off, they said my seizures were too distressing for my friends.

Too distressing for my friends.

Ah yes, because the best way to deal with a chronically ill teenager is to make her feel like a burden to everyone around her. Nice touch, really.

Maybe—just *maybe*—they should've asked my friends what they thought instead of making assumptions. As it turned out, the only thing that distressed *them* was hearing the school administration's opinion of me. When I relayed their comments back, my friends weren't particularly happy they were spoken for. And guess what? I'm still friends with those girls all these years later. They're fine. In fact, they're thriving.

I think they were actually more distressed by the idea that anyone could think I wasn't capable of doing this. I still remember them fighting for me, sitting in the school hallways with me during breaks when I was having a hard time. And yet, here was the school principal, telling me that *my condition* was something to be pitied, something that made me lesser. Spoiler alert: I *did* finish my HSC in one year. I taught myself the circular and I did it my way. And I'm sure my friends would say that the only thing "distressing" about it all was the ridiculous assumptions people made about me.

So, when people today tell me that "it must be hard to keep up with all that work," I just smile. Because I've been defying odds for a long time now. Every time I've been told I couldn't do something, I just pushed harder. That meeting with the principal didn't break me—it *fueled me.* And every time someone tries to tell me I'm not capable of doing something because of my health, I think back to those days. If I could tackle Year 12 with a seizure or two a day, there's not much that can stop me now.

And yes, I *do* get petty about it sometimes. No secrets here—I'll fully admit it. Take my master's graduation, for example. A huge achievement, right? Naturally, I went to post about it on Instagram because, of course, *did it even happen if you don't post it?* (Relax, that's a joke—my Instagram is nothing to draw attention to.) But as I sat there, typing out a caption, I found myself writing: *"This one is dedicated to the high school teachers who didn't think I'd even finish school in one go."*

Oh, the satisfaction. The perfect *mic drop* moment. But then, mid-typing, I stopped and thought— *What's the point?* Like, really. What am I trying to prove? Would some long-forgotten teacher see it and suddenly gasp, *My God, I was wrong! She's amazing!* Doubtful. And even if they did, why should I care?

Sure, it would have been a glorious *chef's kiss* level of pettiness. A nice little *screw you* wrapped in a graduation cap. But at the end of the day, I don't owe them—or anyone—proof of my capabilities. I know what I'm capable of, and that's all that really matters.

Besides, if I really wanted to be petty, I'd name an especially annoying symptom after one of them. Now *that* would be satisfying.

The Two Layers of People: Close Family and the Gossip Circle

There are basically two layers of people in my life. There's the close family who gets the *real* updates— like when my mum calls and casually mentions, "Your sister is in hospital again," as if it's just another Tuesday. You know, the ones who actually *know* what's going on and have been with me through the ups and downs.

Then there's the next layer: the people who hear through the grapevine, like they're waiting for the latest episode of some ongoing drama. These people, when they see me, give me the *most loaded* "How are you?" Like they've clearly heard something and need to hear *all the details*. Seems standard, right? Most people ask how you're doing as a general check-in, and you can throw back something casual like, "I'm good, just busy." That's the polite dance we all do. But no. Not for these people. When I answer, "I'm good," or talk about something *trivial* like how I finally managed to get through my inbox that week or how I'm excited about a new Netflix show I've started, they stop me. They look at me with *that* face. You know the one. It's the face that says, "No, I need more." And then comes the *dramatic* follow-up: *"No, HOW are you?"*

Right. I get it now. So I just stare at them, probably looking as confused as I feel, and clarify, "Yes, I'm good, thank you."

It's like they expect me to be on the brink of some emotional breakdown at any given moment. *Is there an illness-specific handbook that says I have to emotionally unravel in front of them?* Because honestly, I don't think I got that memo.

Here's the thing, though: it's not that I'm hiding my life. It's that I just don't owe anyone *anything*. I don't need to give you a daily dose of my medical rundown. You don't need to know how many more lesions I have or how low my bone density is—unless you're a doctor or someone who genuinely needs to know. And even then, I get to decide *how much* I share. For some reason, people just assume that because I've got a chronic condition, I must be willing to bare it all to satisfy their curiosity. And, like, sure, I get it. People come from a place of concern, but at a certain point, it's just about *being in the know*.

I'm not here to entertain you with the ongoing saga of my health, so let's just agree that if I say I'm good, *I'm good*. No need to dig deeper into the play-by-play of my medical life unless I offer it up. After all, there's a difference between *genuine care* and just wanting to be the first to know the latest gossip.

If You Really Need to Know—Just Ask!

Look, if you're genuinely curious about my health and feel like you *must* know the latest details from my medical charts, you know what? Just ask. I'd much rather you do that than throw around a half-hearted *"How are you?"* that feels more like a formality than an actual interest in my well-being.

Here's the thing: when you ask, "How are you?" but are not actually ready to hear the answer, it comes off as disingenuous. Honestly, it's kind of frustrating when I know you're not really asking about the new hobbies I've started or the weird things I saw on the way to work. You don't want to hear about that crazy street performer I encountered or my obsession with collecting funky coffee mugs—what you really want to know is whether I'm sick, flaring up, or what the latest test results say. And hey, that's fine! It's a part of my life, so if you're truly curious, just ask.

Don't hide behind a generic "How are you?" when

you don't actually care about the other aspects of my life. If you're asking out of real concern or curiosity, then be real about it. Come out and say, *"Hey, I've been thinking about you—how's everything going with your health?"* That's a conversation I'm more than happy to have. It's honest, direct, and respectful.

I know not everyone is comfortable diving into medical details, but if you're close enough to me to care about my health, then just own it. I'm happy to share if I'm in the mood to talk, and you don't have to pretend to care about the other stuff to ask.

So, the next time you're wondering, "How's she really doing?" don't hide it behind the usual, polite "How are you?" Be upfront. I'll respect you more for it, and we'll both be having a real conversation.

The "How Are You?" Conundrum: Lies, Truths, and Everything in Between

Sometimes, before going into events where I know I'm going to be bombarded by well-meaning but overly curious people, my mum gives me the pre-talk: *"Just tell them you're well."* And I get it. I know where she's coming from. She's trying to protect me. She wants me to avoid the unsolicited advice, the pity, and those looks of concern that everyone seems to have a habit of throwing my way when I tell them the truth.

There are two types of responses I give, depending on who's asking.

The 'Really Well' Response: This is the classic go-to. I smile, I stand tall, and I say something like, "I'm really well, thank you! Haven't been sick in ages." This, of course, is a *total* lie. I've probably just vomited up my lunch because I tweaked my medication dosage and went a bit overboard with the portion sizes. But you know what? Sometimes, it's easier to just give them that answer and move on. It's like, *yep, life's great, moving on now.*

The 'Truth Bomb' Response: Then, depending on who it is (and how much I really care about the conversation), sometimes I just tell the truth. No fluff, no sugarcoating. If I'm talking to someone who I trust or who *actually* wants to hear the real deal, I might throw in something about how my bones feel like they're made of glass today or how I'm navigating a flare-up like a pro, but not without a few extra painkillers in the mix.

Here's the thing, though—I can do what I want. I don't have to present some flawless, Instagram-filtered version of myself to anyone. If I'm doing great, I'll say it. If I'm struggling, I'll say it. It's not about keeping some perfect image for the world. Sometimes, yeah, I'm going to lie and tell people everything is fine. Other times, I'm going to be vulnerable and let the truth come out because that's my prerogative.

And you know what? It's okay to let people see me as *human*. Being real isn't a crime, and if I show a bit of vulnerability, that's fine, too. In fact, it's probably easier to be honest than pretending that every day is some flawless walk in the park.

So, thanks, Mum. I know you're looking out for me, but I've learned to walk that line between holding up the "I'm fine" mask and saying, "Hey, it's been tough, but I'm still here." I've got that balance down now. But, you know, no promises, I won't throw in the occasional *really well* just to save myself from yet another round of unsolicited health advice.

"You're Probably Just Stressed"– Well, Aren't We All?

Ah yes, the classic *"You're probably just stressed."* Nothing says *medical expertise* quite like assuming that *everything* can be boiled down to stress. Now, don't get me wrong—I'm no stranger to stress. In fact, stress and I go *way back.* But the real issue here is that little word: just.

Let's acknowledge a crucial distinction—there's mental stress and then there's physical stress. And for me? They are *very* different things. When my body is under physical stress, things go south—fast. Fevers, infections, injuries, full-blown health spirals. My body treats physical stress like an all-you-can-eat buffet of suffering, where it takes everything it can and then *some.* But mental stress? Strangely enough, my body seems to *shrug it off.* If stress alone was the root cause of my health issues, I'd be in the ER every time I had to deal with slow walkers, unexpected phone calls, or remembering all my passwords.

But that's not how my body works. Need proof? Let's talk about holidays, the time when people are *supposed* to be at their most relaxed. I've been on

85

holiday, in my most blissfully stress-free state, fully embracing rest and recovery... and *boom*—hospitalised. (Safe to say, *holiday over.*) The irony? I have also been in *high-stakes, mentally stressful* situations—where any normal person might have been falling apart from sheer pressure—and yet, physically? Perfectly fine. If I could swap the two, I *absolutely* would. Imagine if my body could have a *meltdown* over an existential crisis instead of, say, having to endure a slightly cold breeze. That would be lovely.

And then we have surgery. Ah yes, my body's favourite test of endurance. The first time, we had no idea what we were in for. Pre-surgery? I was *stressed.* Nervous, anxious, borderline freaking out. But physically? Totally fine. Then post-surgery? Oh, *that's* when things got interesting. I hadn't even woken up from the anaesthetic when the seizures started. Fifteen convulsions. Mind you, I was still *unconscious.* There was *zero* mental stress involved—my brain wasn't even in the game yet. And yet, my body? Fully committed to the chaos.

And that's the reality of my condition—it doesn't follow the rules people *think* it should. I could be lying on a beach, sipping a mocktail, reading a book, and my body could suddenly decide it's time for an emergency room visit. Or I could be dealing with a massively stressful situation where any *reasonable* person's health might take a hit, and I'd be completely *fine*. If my illness was simply stress-related, I could *meditate it away*, book a spa day, or slap on some essential oils and call it a cure. But we all know that's not how it works.

So, for the *know-it-alls* who love to confidently diagnose me with *stress* as the root of all my problems—no, you're wrong. Again. But thanks for playing.

Like I said, I do get my fair dose of stress and there are a few psychologists all over. You know what's ironic? And, honestly, kind of poetic? I now see a therapist named *Dave*. A *different* Dave, obviously. But still. What are the odds?

And here's the kicker—I *actually* like this Dave. In fact, I think he's fantastic. My first ever male psychologist since *THAT* one, and he just so happens to have the same name. It's like life decided to throw me into a weird, twisted version of exposure therapy, but with a plot twist: I *enjoy* talking to him.

Talk about a healing process. Full-circle moment? *Check.* Personal growth? *Double check.* The universe having an absolutely unhinged sense of humour? *Triple check.* At this point, I wouldn't even be surprised if my next doctor is named Albert or Terry.

Caught Off Guard: The Art of Not Knowing What to Say

I'm not exactly someone who does well under pressure if caught off guard. You know that moment when someone says something so *astonishingly bad* that you're just left staring at them like a deer in headlights? Yeah, that's me. I get hit with those comments a lot, and I swear, every time, I just freeze. It's like my brain short-circuits. The words I'm supposed to say... gone. The snarky comeback I've been rehearsing in my head for the past 15 years? *Poof.*

And here's the thing: for someone who doesn't do well in these situations, you'd think I'd manage to avoid them more often. Nope! They keep coming, like a weird game of "Guess What Horrible Thing Someone's Gonna Say to You Today." Spoiler alert: it's usually something along the lines of, "So, I am guessing you won't live very long." Comments I'm absolutely *not* prepared for. So, I stand there, trying to process the absurdity of it all, and the only thing I can muster is a confused look. What do you even say to that? Do I sit there and educate them about chronic illness, or do I just smile and nod like I'm in some terrible, never-ending sitcom?

If I had to think back to the most shocking question I've ever been asked, it would be on two separate occasions—by people I'm not particularly close to—who, out of nowhere, asked me if my heart issues make it problematic for me to have sex. Yes, you read that right. May I just add that these people weren't asking because they needed to know—they were genuinely curious. *Genuinely curious.* They received a blank, very shook stare in response. How exactly do you respond to that?

It's one thing to be asked about your health, but it's another when someone feels so comfortable as to inquire about your sex life in the most inappropriate way possible. But hey, I guess we can add "awkward conversation starter" to the list of things I never saw coming. In those moments, I'm basically a walking mime. I could have a *brilliant* response in my head 10 minutes later, but in that moment, all I do is stare and blink as if trying to remember my own name. Seriously, it's like my brain has a 'No Functioning' sign on it when I'm faced with the truly *bizarre* things people say.

So, yeah, that's where I am. Trapped in a loop of having to come up with clever comebacks... but always too late. It's a real talent, honestly. You'd think by now I'd be used to it, but somehow, it still gets me every single time. Maybe one day, I'll just start carrying around a list of responses on a laminated card. "What do you say when someone needs a life lesson on common sense?"

There's a certain kind of comment that really knows how to *stop you dead in your tracks*. It's not the usual "How are you?" or the "You don't look sick" that gets under your skin because you've heard those a million times. No, it's the big guns. The ones that make you blink, stare, and internally wonder if you've just entered some alternate reality where people forget to use filters. Take this gem for example: *"So, I'm guessing you won't live very long."*

Yeah. Someone actually said that to me. I mean, just let that sink in for a moment. That's not a "Hey, how's your health?" or "How are you feeling?" Oh no. That's straight-up, take-no-prisoners, *"Oh, you're probably going to die soon, huh?"* The kind of thing that, for about three seconds, makes you think, *Did they seriously just say that?* And the worst part? I was so stunned that I didn't even know how to respond. In that moment, I wasn't prepared for this... *dark prophecy* that someone was casually throwing my way like it was a weather forecast. "Chance of rain: 40%. Chance of your early demise: 100%."

My mind went blank. Was I supposed to laugh it off? Cry? I mean, how do you even react to something like that? *Do I ask for a refund for the awkwardness?* Do I say, "No, actually, I'm planning on living a nice long life; thank you for your *cheerful* prognosis!?"

But here's the thing: people like that. They don't even get to have a say in my story. It's wild how people think they can just throw out these big, heavy assumptions about you without considering the impact of their words. And let's be clear: there's no *right* way to respond to something like that. Sometimes, you're left standing there wondering if you're in some weird, dystopian movie, trying to figure out how to react to the absurdity of the situation. At the end of the day, I guess what I've learned is this: *I'm still here.* So, while that person may have made a dramatic guess about my future, I'm over here living my life, one day at a time. And, spoiler alert: it's still going.

If they ask again, I'll just hit them with a simple: "Actually, I'm doing just fine, and I plan on sticking around a lot longer than your assumption." That should be enough to leave them speechless for once.

Okay, just to clarify—*one more time for the people in the back*—my autoimmune condition does NOT impact my life expectancy. Yes, that's true. I'm not working with a ticking clock here. No need for dramatic music or dystopian death scenes. My condition may mess with my body in a thousand ways, but it isn't writing my obituary anytime soon. That's a little thing called *facts*. Still, there's always that one person who thinks they have the right to comment on my lifespan with the subtlety of a sledgehammer. Case in point: *"So, I'm guessing you won't live very long."*

Let me just take a moment to really drive this home—*my autoimmune condition doesn't make me some walking expiration date*. So, the next time someone feels the need to share their *expert* predictions on my health, I'm just going to hand them a nice little card that says, "Thanks for your concern. I'm still going strong—expecting many more years ahead."

To anyone out there ready to throw out a doomsday scenario: I'm good. And spoiler alert 101, I'm living my life *as I please*. You can keep the medical guesses to yourself.

The Blood Clot Debacle: A Very Special Episode of "How Not to Help"

I'll never forget when I got my blood clot. Yeah, you read that right—a deep vein thrombosis in my internal jugular vein. It was about 3 cm long, and the doctors were very clear: *If it dislodged, I'd block my airway instantly.* You know, no pressure. Just a casual, life-or-death situation, nothing to be concerned about. They told me I couldn't do things for months: no lifting my arm above my head, no climbing stairs, no walking too fast—basically, no fun allowed.

To be honest, I was well aware of the gravity of the situation, but I took it in stride. It was a pickle, for sure, but one I could manage. I was 19, and even though I didn't exactly want to *die* from a blood clot, I wasn't going to let it rule my life. I made the necessary adjustments, took care of myself, and did what I had to do. *Life continued.*

Here's another kicker—if I had a dollar for every person who *felt the need* to remind me that the blood clot could kill me, I'd be sipping cocktails on a private island somewhere, living the dream. It's like, sure, *I know* it could kill me. I'm not exactly walking around with a blindfold on and a "Who cares?!" attitude. But apparently, everyone else felt it was their job to add their two cents, making sure I was well aware of the potential "instant death" scenario.

I'd be sitting in class, or at a social event, or just out in the world, and someone would casually drop the line, "You know, that clot could kill you, right?" Thanks, Karen, I didn't know! Here I was thinking I was just casually carrying around a glorified *thrombosis souvenir* for the fun of it. Appreciate the reminder.

And it wasn't just once; it was a steady stream of concerned faces offering up their grim predictions as if I hadn't heard them already. It's like they had a *script*—and honestly, I think they all rehearsed it in front of the mirror just in case they got the chance to say it.

It's one thing to be cautious, and it's another to make a 19-year-old feel like they're living on borrowed time every time they step out the door. I get that people care, but good grief, maybe tone it down a little? Sometimes, *just maybe*, it's not about reminding me of the worst-case scenario. Sometimes, it's about *letting me be* and not treating me like I'm walking around with a ticking time bomb strapped to my neck. Nonetheless, I survived.

If I had a dollar for every person who casually reminded me of how I could've died, I'd have a retirement fund big enough to never work again. But hey, the things people think they need to say! If you ever want to feel alive, try getting a health scare and watching the world's unsolicited commentary come at you from all angles. You'll probably think, *"Oh god, I can't say anything right."* And honestly, I get it. Sometimes, the words just fly out of your mouth before you've had a chance to think. It happens. But maybe we can try an experiment. Let's see if we can find some things that are actually helpful and not... well, rude.

Take, for instance, when I tell you about something serious like a blood clot. I get it—someone drops that bombshell on you, and you're shocked. Maybe you're rattled by how calm I seem (or appear to seem). You've just heard something that shakes you, and your brain scrambles for the right words. But what comes out is *probably* not going to be what I want to hear. And, in all fairness, I know you didn't mean to sound insensitive—it's just one of those things where the first thing that pops into your head doesn't always come out the right way. So, here's a suggestion: *"Wow, that sounds like a lot, how are you feeling?"* Simple. Direct.

Compassionate. It acknowledges what I've just shared without making me feel like I need to either laugh it off or brush it under the rug.

What if I *am* having nightmares every night? What if I'm scared to run up the stairs because I'm worried the blood clot might dislodge and turn into a pulmonary embolism? What if I'm panicking on the inside but trying to keep it together on the outside because, well, *what else can I do?* What if I'm just looking for someone to ask me how I'm really feeling without jumping straight to their own shock or offering advice I didn't ask for?

Sometimes, all I need is for someone to *see me—* really see me—and ask, *"How are you feeling?"* without the pressure to either minimise the situation or turn it into a "problem" that needs fixing.

So, next time you're faced with something heavy or unexpected, remember: it's okay to be shocked. It's okay to not have all the answers. But just be real, be kind, and ask, *"How are you feeling?"* That's a start.

The Bedside Manner That Wasn't

Some of the things I've heard from doctors and nurses over the years... well, let's just say they're *shocking*—in the worst way. Sure, some medical professionals are amazing, but others? Not so much. They sometimes lacked empathy or even basic human understanding.

I remember being about 20 years old, lying in a hospital bed in the middle of one of my most challenging flare-ups. I wasn't on steroids yet, and my brain was basically on fire, struggling to function. I couldn't string a sentence together properly, I was having constant seizures, and things were *not* going well. One night, I had a seizure and because the hospital bed's side rails weren't up, I fell right out. I woke up on the floor, dazed and buzzing the nurse. I was crying, trying to explain what had happened, and you could see the confusion in her eyes. She didn't seem to know how to react.

She asked, "Do you want painkillers?"

"No," I said, shaking my head, still a little out of it.

She looked at me, *utterly perplexed*, and said, "Well... what do you want then?"

I didn't want painkillers. I didn't want anything *medical.* I wasn't thinking about my body or my symptoms—I just wanted someone to *care.* What I wanted, what I really needed, was my mum. I wanted a hug. I wanted comfort, warmth, something to make me feel human again in the midst of the chaos. I didn't need to be a patient on a chart with a number beside my name. I needed a person to acknowledge the *emotional* side of what I was going through. I was more than just a medical case.

Instead, I got the cold, clinical response: a nurse confused by my lack of desire for painkillers and a feeling of being treated like one more body to manage. *A patient.* A number on a list. At the end of the day, patients aren't just numbers. We're not just walking conditions to be fixed. We have feelings, needs, emotions. It's a real shame that in a place where we should feel the most cared for, we can sometimes feel most lonely.

I don't know much about what it takes to train to be a nurse, but surely rapport building is part of the curriculum, right? I mean, I would think that being able to connect with a patient, especially in moments of fear or stress, would be an essential part of the job. Based on a few experiences I've had,

I'm not always convinced that this is being taught as thoroughly as it should be. I've had some truly fantastic nurses over the years, and for the most part, they've been amazing—compassionate, professional, and understanding. But, I have to be honest, the ones who haven't been so great? Well, let's just say they've left quite an impression, and not in a good way.

I'm setting aside the actual medical practice for now, because that's a whole different ballgame, and focusing just on the commentary—the things that get said while you're vulnerable, in pain, or just trying to make it through the day. Now, you might think, *"Okay, that was just one nurse."* Fair enough, I get it. But that wasn't just one moment in time—it was one of the most memorable occasions of a pattern. Let me share a story with you.

I've got quite a high pain tolerance, and I guess a lot of that comes from years of desensitisation. When you deal with chronic illness, you sort of become accustomed to pain and discomfort. But here's the thing—pain and the unknown aren't always the same thing. When I have to undergo a new test, one I've never had before, I usually get quite nervous. It's not the pain I'm afraid of—it's the *unknown*. The lack of control over a situation is what gets me every time.

I remember one time, I was in the hospital for ten days, going through back-to-back scans and tests, each one more invasive than the last. It was one of those endless days where every new procedure just felt like a wave crashing over me. Then came the lumbar puncture day. For those who don't know, lumbar puncture is when they insert a needle into your spine to draw out cerebrospinal fluid. It's not the best feeling, and for a lot of people, it can be a really scary experience.

I was young, nervous, and completely dreading it. I had no idea what to expect, and that unknown was what made me feel like I was spiralling. Finally, the moment arrived. The nurses came into the room, and you know what they said? *"Yeah, it's gonna hurt."* Wait, what? *What did you just say?* Instant panic. I mean, seriously? That's your comforting message, right before you stick two needles in my spine? Suddenly, my mind was flooded with a hundred "what ifs" that were spinning out of control.

To be fair, I'm sure they were just trying to prepare me for the discomfort. But, telling a patient *"it's gonna hurt"* without any reassurance, without any attempt to comfort them or explain what's happening, is the exact opposite of rapport building. It's more like a trigger for all of my anxieties and fears to run wild. It might seem small to someone on the other side of the needle, but to me, it felt like the whole world was crashing down in that moment.

Since then, I've had a couple more lumbar punctures, and over time, I've learned to handle them without panic. But that initial experience? It still sticks with me. It wasn't just the procedure; it was the lack of empathy in the way it was delivered. Nurses, doctors, healthcare professionals—they have the power to calm a storm or make it worse with just a few words. Rapport building isn't just about technical knowledge; it's about understanding where the patient is coming from emotionally and mentally. It's about offering comfort and clear, empathetic communication.

Sometimes, those comments can make a huge impact—more than we're willing to admit, especially when we're already feeling vulnerable. It's not that we're not thankful for the care we receive, but sometimes, a little more thoughtfulness in the way things are said can go a long way. So, next time you're in a position to help someone through a difficult moment—whether you're a nurse, a doctor, or even just a friend—remember that what you say can have a lasting impact. Instead of just bluntly telling me that something's going to hurt, maybe try, *"This might be uncomfortable, but we're here with you, and we'll do everything we can to make it as easy as possible."* That's how you build rapport, and that's how you make a difficult experience just a little bit easier to bear.

The Perils of "New Doctor, Same Story"

Whenever I find myself in the emergency department, I get to meet a fresh crop of doctors who are usually fascinated by my case. I'm like a *medical mystery* they can't wait to unpack. They look at me with that eager, wide-eyed curiosity as if they're about to crack some sort of code that's eluded everyone else. And, of course, they want to run more tests, explore all the angles, and get *very* scientific about it.

I totally get why that happens. At one point, one of my doctors even started calling me an "enigma" because I had this never-ending, constantly evolving list of symptoms that they just couldn't quite piece together. It became this weird kind of puzzle for them—fascinating, almost like a medical mystery. Of course, that was from their perspective. For me, living with it day in and day out wasn't so much fascinating as it was exhausting.

I get it—when you're trying to figure out what's going on with someone's health and nothing seems to fit neatly into place, it can be perplexing. But sometimes, when you're the one in the middle of all those "mysteries," it doesn't feel so much like a puzzle to be solved as it does a game of "how much more can you take?" I know they weren't trying to make light of my situation, but sometimes it felt like my chronic, ever-changing symptoms were just a bit too much for them to handle. It's a fine line between curiosity and empathy, and not everyone manages to strike the balance.

So, I'd show up at the emergency department, and without fail, that same fascination would kick in. The questions would start pouring in, and I could almost hear the "Hmm, this is interesting" vibe coming from their tone. I get it—being a doctor, you deal with a lot of complex cases, and sometimes, when you're presented with something that doesn't make sense, it becomes this intellectual challenge. But let me tell you, it's a little disorienting when you're the one dealing with a body that feels like it's falling apart, and you sense that kind of fascination rather than empathy. It's like, okay, I'm glad you find me fascinating, but could we maybe focus on the part where I'm in pain and not just on the mystery of my symptoms?

Except, there's always one little problem: I've been in this show *before*. Repeatedly. The plot is so familiar that I could probably write the script by now. But, naturally, no one listens to the patient who's been *living* this saga for years. Take, for example, a little adventure during COVID. My doctor had me go to the ER, as the virus had triggered a flare-up of my autoimmune condition. My lungs were wheezing badly—nothing new, just the usual response to my body stress. I needed my standard rescue puffs, a bit of extra steroids, and the usual treatment.

However, the doctor, who didn't know me and apparently had a very different idea of what was going on, was convinced my issue wasn't what it had already been diagnosed to be. He was *sure* there was some mysterious physical blockage in my throat. I was *struggling* to breathe through the night, gasping for air. Meanwhile, the nurse, who clearly understood how things worked better than the doctor, would sneak behind the curtain to give me my Ventolin when he wasn't there so that the wheezing would settle.

Though I'm pretty sure she wasn't actually allowed to go against the doctor's orders, I couldn't help but notice that it was the only thing that seemed to be getting me through the night. And even with those occasional puffs of Ventolin here and there, it still wasn't quite cutting it. It wasn't even close to the level of relief I'd typically get when I was sent to the hospital for a flare-up in my lungs. I'd almost gotten used to those flare-ups, and while they were terrifying, I knew what to expect. But this? This was different. The medication was just a temporary fix—it didn't even come close to what I needed to feel like I was actually getting better. And while I could sense the fascination around me, I just wished that same energy could be put into making me feel better rather than making me feel like I was some sort of medical enigma.

By morning, the doctor's boss showed up, took one look at the situation, and immediately corrected his colleague's "theory." They put me back on the Ventolin, gave me oxygen and the steroids I had originally stated were needed. Turns out—shockingly enough—the patient *was right*.

Honestly, it's like living in a medical version of "Groundhog Day." The same mistakes, the same reassurances, the same moment where I'm proven correct, and the doctors learn what I've known all along. I'm not a doctor, but I *do* have a bit of expertise on how my body works. And yet, in the ER, it's like I have to fight for that recognition every single time.

In the end, it was a win for me. But also—can someone please tell these doctors that maybe listening to the patient who's been living with their body for years might save us all some time?

The Silver Lining: My Amazing Medical Team

Now, I have to admit—after many years of navigating the confusing, often frustrating world of autoimmune disorders, I *do* have an amazing team of doctors. Seriously! If I had a nickel for every time they've helped me or made me feel heard, I'd have a small fortune by now. They've been with me through the highs and lows, the confusing processes, and the endless tests that made me wonder if they're just making things up as they go. These doctors, nurses, and specialists? They've been *the real MVPs*.

I mean, yes, I've had some truly ridiculous moments where I've had to explain things over and over, answer the same questions for the hundredth time, or *gently* correct the occasional "misstep" from well-meaning medical professionals. In the end, my team gets it. They've been there, understanding my condition in all its nuance, and treating me with both expertise and empathy. It's not always perfect, of course. Who's perfect in healthcare? But I've reached a point where I genuinely trust my doctors and definitely my nurses.

Despite the ups and downs of my medical journey, there's one constant that's been a real saving grace: every four weeks for the last four-ish years, I go to the hospital for an infusion. For about four hours, I sit in a chair, hooked up to an IV, letting the medication do its thing. Every time I walk into that infusion room, my nurses greet me with genuine *happiness*. It's not just a routine check-in; it's a moment where I feel like a person again, not just a patient. There's always a smile, a warm welcome, and a little bit of lightness in the air that helps make those long hours a bit more bearable.

I don't think they realise how much of a difference it makes. It's not just about the medical procedure—it's the way they make me feel cared for. Those small moments of kindness, a nurse asking how my week's been or joking about something trivial, turn what could be a gruelling experience into something just a little bit easier to endure.

In a world where I've been treated like a set of symptoms, numbers, and test results, those nurses are the ones who remind me that I'm still a human being—someone worthy of kindness, attention, and care. They make the whole process feel a little less lonely. These moments, these small acts of warmth, can truly change the way a person feels in a hospital room. I'll take that every time.

So if you ever feel like you're not being heard by your medical team—or worse, that they're subtly (or not so subtly) implying it's *all in your head*—let me be clear: *they aren't your people.* I hear so many people say, *"Well, you know how it is,"* when talking about the struggles of the healthcare system, as if frustration and dismissal are just part of the package. But no. That's not just *how it is*. That's just *not your team*. And trust me—I've been there.

Now that I've finally found a team of doctors who actually *gel* with me, I realise just how important it is to keep searching until you find the *right* people. And it's not about labelling doctors as "good" or "bad"—it's about finding the ones that fit *you*. The ones who listen. The ones who *get* it. The ones who don't make you feel like a burden for advocating for yourself.

And let me tell you—*they are out there.* You deserve a team that works *with* you, not against you. So keep looking. Keep pushing. Because when you find the right people, the difference is *life-changing.*

The Weight Comment That No One Asked For

After every trip to the hospital, I tend to lose a fair amount of weight. I'm not sure exactly why it happens—maybe because of the stress on my body or just one of the side effects of everything I've been through. But every time it does happen, people seem to feel it's their duty to point it out. Just to clarify, I'm not talking about spending a single night in emergency; I'm talking about anything upward of a week-long stay.

I'm pretty sure there's this unspoken rule in society: *don't comment on someone's weight.* Whether you think someone has gained or lost a few kilos, unless you're their doctor or nutritionist, it's generally considered bad manners to bring it up. Apparently, that rule doesn't apply to me.

"Wow, you're looking *so* skinny. Don't lose any more weight!" people will say.

Thanks for the update, I guess?

Here's the thing: I'm not hitting the gym and sweating it out on the treadmill every chance I get. Trust me, if I could, I would. Unfortunately, my body isn't exactly a fan of those kinds of activities. So when I lose weight, it's usually because of something I have zero control over. And yeah, it makes me self-conscious. I'm already dealing with a lot, so the last thing I need is people pointing out something that's already noticeable. It's like no one ever stops to think, "Hmm, maybe this person doesn't want to talk about their weight right now." Instead, they just throw it out there as if I don't already know. When you live with an autoimmune condition or any chronic illness, your body is constantly changing in ways you can't predict or control. So, while I know it's usually said out of *concern*, it doesn't exactly make me feel any better.

If anything, it just reminds me that no matter what's going on in my life, I'll always be the one who's *too skinny*, *too tired*, or *too sick* for everyone else's liking. Sometimes, I just want to be left to handle my own body the way I see fit. If I'm looking withdrawn and pale, there's really no need to keep pointing it out. Yes, I know. Believe me, I've seen myself in the mirror. I can tell when I'm looking a little off, and trust me, I don't need anyone to remind me. It's like this weird, unspoken rule that when someone is visibly unwell, people feel the need to reiterate the obvious like it's some kind of revelation.

There was a stage when I started a new immunosuppressant, and let's just say—my body was *not* a fan. In fact, it rejected it with the same enthusiasm I reject unsolicited medical advice. I was on this medication for far too many months, and during that time, my daily routine included throwing up about six times a day, like clockwork. Every single piece of food I swallowed made a swift return as if my stomach had a strict "no entry" policy. Naturally, the weight was coming off *fast*. And that's when the comments came flying in.

"Wow, you look really pale today!"

"You are too skinny."

"You look very tired."

No kidding. I'm aware. If being honest, pointing it out doesn't exactly help. In fact, it just draws more attention to how not okay I'm feeling, and after hearing it over and over, it starts to feel like a broken record. And frankly, considering I was spending most of my day in an intimate, borderline *romantic* relationship with my toilet bowl, my weight was the *least* of my problems.

I get it—people are trying to be caring, trying to be observant. But sometimes, it's like you're just stating the thing I'm already painfully aware of. What would be way more helpful than pointing out the obvious is *just being there*—without having to make it a headline. Sometimes, the last thing I want to hear is someone commenting on how sick I look. It's like saying, *"Hey, I noticed you're struggling, let me highlight that for everyone to see!"*

So, just a heads-up: If I look withdrawn or pale, I'm probably already feeling pretty awful, and I don't need anyone to give me a weekly update on my appearance. Let's focus on the things that *really* matter instead. It's all about not making it worse by making it the centre of attention.

The "Once" Experience

Alright, I know this one might ruffle a few feathers, but just a reminder—this isn't a personal attack, it's all about raising awareness. As I mentioned, I rarely have seizures these days—probably just one a year—but over the last decade, we've cycled through a whole series of "stages." First, it was the "once a week" stage, then "three times a week," followed by "eight times a week" (because, of course, that was the peak). Then it settled into "once a month," "three months apart," "a few times a year," and now we've reached the "on special occasions" phase. When you add them all up, we're comfortably in the thousands. That's thousands of seizures.

Yet, every time I tell someone about the seizures I've had, there's always *that person* who says, "Oh, yeah, I know *exactly* what it's like for you. I passed out once."

Really? *Once? And you know exactly what it's like.* I mean, don't get me wrong—being unconscious sucks. It's a whole thing, and I get it, but let's not pretend it's the same thing as daily seizures. And then someone says, "Oh yeah, I've fainted before. That's basically the same thing, right?"

I mean, sure, I guess we were both unconscious—but let's not get carried away. Telling me you once fainted doesn't exactly make me feel *seen* just because we both briefly checked out. So, what do I say to that? "Welcome to the club?" As if we're now in the same category because they fainted once and I've had to deal with *this* for over a decade?

Honestly, I just want to say nope... shhh... not the same. And just to be clear, I don't mean to sound unempathetic. When I'm actually speaking to someone, I don't respond like this. I check in, ask what the experience was like for them, and explore the topic—because if they've brought it up, there's a reason for it. However, it can be *incredibly* draining when people assume they can relate. I get that it often comes from a good place—people want to connect, to show empathy, to find common ground. But at the end of the day, whether you've had one seizure or a thousand, no one can truly understand what someone else is going through.

That one seizure might have been *terrifying* for that person, and I'm not here to downplay that in the slightest. Trauma is trauma, and everyone's experience is valid. But experiencing something *once* doesn't mean you suddenly understand the full scope of what it's like to live with it *constantly*. It's the difference between visiting a foreign country for a week and actually living there. Sure, you got a taste of it, but you didn't have to learn the language, navigate the system long-term, or rebuild your entire life around it.

So, while I appreciate the effort to relate, there's a fine line between empathy and assumption. And honestly? Sometimes, the best way to show support isn't by saying, *"I know exactly how you feel,"* but by acknowledging that you *don't*—and just being willing to listen instead.

Faking a Seizure? That's *Definitely* a New One

Okay, this one always cracks me up. Many people have *actually* said to me, "Surely you've faked a seizure to get out of doing something you don't want to do."

Now, first of all, I don't know what kind of social events they think I'm attending to want to get out of, but apparently, I've been missing out on the *"How to Fake a Seizure for Dummies"* guide. Let's be real: I've never actually seen someone have a seizure, and even if I had, how in the world would I know what I'm supposed to do? I'm already dealing with the whole "being sick" thing, and now I'm supposed to master *acting* sick? Can we just take a moment to acknowledge how absurd that is?

Look, I get it. The idea of faking a seizure to avoid something like a *family gathering* or a *dreadful social event* might sound like a *great* escape plan. I'd love the ability to magically bow out of things I don't want to do. *"Oh, I can't go to that dinner...oh look, I'm having a seizure right now! Oops!"* But the problem is, I wouldn't even know where to start.

Do I just flop to the ground like a rag-doll and

hope for the best? Like, "Yeah, just gonna fall right now, like I'm a bag of potatoes and completely lose control of my body, totally believable, right?" No. First off, I don't think I could pull off the *drop like a bag of potatoes* part because—*ouch!*—that's gotta hurt. I mean, I can barely manage to trip over my own feet, let alone intentionally drop to the floor without breaking something.

As someone who has dislocated limbs in a fall and *not even flinched*, I can assure you if I were to take a fall with *that* much force while simultaneously putting on an Oscar-worthy performance, that would be some next-level talent. We're talking *method acting* levels of commitment. So, let's be clear: I'm not out here faking seizures to get out of doing anything. Honestly, if I could get out of social events, I'd just say, *"Hey, I'm really tired and not feeling great today, can I skip this one?"* No need for drama or dramatic falling to the floor.

If anything, I'm the person who *downplays* the issue rather than exaggerating it. I've had seizures and still gone back to school, work, and social events like it's just another Tuesday. I've carried on with my day while my lungs wheeze like an old accordion and my oxygen levels drop or powered through housework with a limp like it's a *perfectly normal* thing to do. So, the idea that I'd suddenly start *faking* seizures... for what reason, exactly? For fun? For the drama? Trust me, seizures are not a party trick—they bring enough challenges into my life already. Why on earth would I *want* more? It's not like I'm waking up every day thinking, *Hmm, you know what would make this day more exciting? An unpredictable medical emergency!*

People don't fake things that actively make their lives harder. If anything, I'm more likely to *minimise* what I'm going through than to put on some grand performance. I've learned life is already complicated enough without adding unnecessary theatrics. And if anyone ever seriously thinks faking a seizure sounds like a good idea, just know: I'm sticking to the *not-so-glamorous* reality of my health, thank you very much. It's way less stressful and much more, well... realistic!

Mind Over Matter? Oh, If Only.

Ah, "mind over matter"—one of those phrases people throw around when they think they've cracked the code to life's struggles. I get it. It sounds empowering. Like, "Hey, if you just *think* hard enough, you can make anything better!" But, let's be honest, if it was that simple, I'd be walking around pain-free, seizure-free, and probably doing yoga at sunrise while sipping my kale smoothie.

People who get seizures often experience something called an *aura*—a warning sign before the seizure hits. For some, it's a weird taste, a flash of light, or even a sudden sense of déjà vu. For me, though? It's a whole sensory overload situation. The room starts to feel like it's closing in on me, sounds turn into a wall of white noise, and my brain just gets *overloaded* with stimuli. In those moments, if I could've told my brain, "Nope, not today, I'm going to *mind over matter* this thing," I would've. I was *literally* saying, "Oh no, not again!" in my head, but guess what? That didn't work because mind over matter doesn't always work when your body is just, well, *not cooperating.*

Now, don't get me wrong—I *do* believe in mind over matter to an extent. There are definitely moments where mental strength helps. Like when you wake up in pain and still have to drag yourself out of bed to go to work (and then go through the whole "pretend to be a functional human being" routine). But the whole "mind over matter" thing gets used *way* too much and often out of context, especially when people are trying to oversimplify complex health issues.

Take, for example, the time I was admitted to the epilepsy ward for a week of EEG (electroencephalogram) monitoring. This was back in the dark days when no one had a clue what was actually going on with me. I spent a week hooked up to electrodes, hoping they would catch something, anything, to explain these episodes.

But, surprise, surprise—because I *don't* have epilepsy, and because I didn't have a seizure while all the electrodes were attached to my head (because, you know, that's how it works), they didn't see any seizure activity on the monitor. So, what did I get at the end of this delightful stay? Two doctors, clipboards in hand, standing at the end of my bed with the solemn expression of someone about to deliver the most profound news ever. And then, the moment that makes me shake my head even now: they told me there was "nothing physically wrong" with me.

Wait, it gets better. They then proceeded to give me the most *patronising* step-by-step tutorial on the concept of "mind over matter." As if *that* was going to be the magic answer. I wish I could've just said, "Oh, really? So, if I just think harder, the seizures will just stop? I never thought of that. I must've missed the memo where I become the master of my own brainwaves."

Here's the thing: *mind over matter* doesn't work when there's something physically going on with your body that you can't control. It's like telling someone with a broken leg, "Just think positive and walk it off." Not exactly helpful. I'd love to have the ability to control every aspect of my health just by thinking hard enough, but sadly, that's not how chronic illness works.

So, to all the well-meaning people out there who throw around the "mind over matter" line—take a seat. It's one of those things that sounds *great* in theory, but in practice, it's way more complicated than just thinking positive thoughts. If only life was that simple, huh?

Pills, Oils, and Empathy: A Daily Dose of Reality

Every morning, without fail, I wake up and swallow fourteen tablets. Then, of course, there are the extras at night, because who doesn't love a good pill regimen to end the day? And let's not forget the painkillers, anti-inflammatories, and anti-nausea meds scattered throughout the day, like little life-saving confetti. These little pills serve a range of purposes: steroids to keep me from crumbling into a heap, meds to stop seizures, others to slow my heart, and a few that basically take my immune system and put it on an eternal vacation.

Without these meds, my daily life would look a lot more... limited. Forget about maintaining a job, living independently, or just getting through a normal day without wondering if I'll collapse. In fact, if I catch a simple stomach bug and the meds exit my body—well, that could easily end in a seizure. But hey, I just keep taking them, right? Logical, sure. And yet, despite the fact that they literally keep my body from falling apart, there always seems to be someone who insists that I should ditch the pills and "go natural" with essential oils or other alternative remedies.

Deep breath... yes, I respect the power of natural health strategies, but let's be real. When your immune system has decided that your own body is the enemy, no amount of eucalyptus oil is going to calm things down. It's not like a nice lavender-scented diffuser is going to convince my body to stop attacking itself.

There was a time when my lungs decided to throw daily tantrums. Wheezing, gasping for air, oxygen levels dropping faster than my patience, and turning a little too blue for my liking—because who doesn't enjoy a good dramatic health scare now and then, right? In those moments, the only thing that could help was a frantic mix of Ventolin puffs, steroids, and—if I was lucky—some old-school, homemade remedies. One of my favourites? Two heaping scoops of Vicks vapour rub in a bowl of boiling water, draping a towel over my head like some makeshift spa treatment, and inhaling deeply. I'm not going to lie, it worked wonders to open up my airways. I'd sit there, feeling the menthol blast through me like I was in a steam room with a very questionable smell. But here's the twist: once I started on new, stronger medications, those attacks stopped. Just like that. It wasn't the Vicks. It wasn't the Ventolin. It was the prescription drugs. See where I'm going with this?

Don't get me wrong—non-medicinal remedies can be fantastic, and I'm all for finding what works for your body. But there's a time and place for everything. People seem to forget that when it comes to health, everyone's body is different. While some may swear by their oils, herbs, and ancient remedies, those things simply aren't going to cut it for me when my immune system is staging a rebellion or my lungs are on strike. I don't need a comment about how I "shouldn't rely on pharmaceuticals" because, well, guess what? These meds are the reason I can breathe, function, and actually live my life. The point here isn't that everyone should be popping pills. The point is that people should keep their opinions to themselves because their bodies don't have the same struggles or requirements as mine. So next time someone offers me advice about how I should "heal naturally," maybe they should take a moment to consider what might be the alternative before they assume their remedy is the answer for everyone.

Before I started this medication cocktail, it felt like playing Russian roulette with my organs. Every year, a new system would break down, leaving me wondering what would go next. Now? I'm stable. Well, stable-ish. I have a routine and a sense of control. But I'll never forget a particular family gathering when I was struggling with pain in my joints after a long day of standing in the humidity. I finally sat down, rummaged through my bag, found some anti-inflammatories, and took them, hoping to get some relief. And that's when it happened—the look. You know the one, the judgmental "You're poisoning your body with all that stuff" look. And here's the kicker: it wasn't from someone who actually needs medication. Oh no, it was from the person who can breeze through a family event without so much as a limp or a second thought. Someone who doesn't know what it's like to fight your body every day, someone who gets to complain about nothing more than being tired from a long lunch.

So, I have to ask: where's the empathy? Where's the understanding? I get there's a strong anti-pharmaceutical movement out there, and I agree that natural remedies can be helpful in some cases. But when you're dealing with something like an autoimmune disease, where your own immune system is hell-bent on self-destruction, the alternative to medication isn't just "natural"—it's far, far worse. It's the pain. It's the daily fight. It's the uncertainty. And sometimes, that little pill is the only thing standing between me and a much darker, much less functional version of life. Maybe I'm "poisoning" my body with my meds, at least I'm still here to feel it.

The Public Spectacle That Is My Immune System

Some people like to keep their private lives, well... private. I am one of those people. At least, I try to be. The issue is, my immune system missed that memo and insists on making a grand spectacle of itself at the worst possible times. It's as if my body is an extrovert while my soul is an introvert, and unfortunately, my body always wins.

Take, for example, the time I started a new job and told myself, *This time, no one needs to know anything. I will just be a mysterious, illness-free enigma.* A solid plan, right? Well, that lasted about as long as it took for my lungs to start performing a symphony mid-shift.

There I was, working away, feeling a little off but nothing dramatic, when I noticed people looking around, confused. Some tilted their heads like curious puppies. Others frowned in concern. What was this strange, otherworldly noise they were hearing? A ghost? A malfunctioning machine? A whale call? No. It was just me and my melodious lungs, gurgling away like an undersea orchestra.

Naturally, I was oblivious because I had my headphones in. When I finally took them off, I was greeted with the beautiful harmony of *Gurgle-Gasp-Wheeze in D Minor*. Suddenly, I was the main character in a scene I never auditioned. Cue embarrassment. Cue swift retreat to find my Ventolin. Cue the inevitable onslaught of people wanting to know what happened. Before you know it, my entire medical history was public domain. Again. So much for privacy.

Fast forward to the next job. *This time will be different,* I told myself. *No singing lungs, no medical mysteries, just work.* But, as always, my immune system laughed in my face. Maybe it was a seizure, maybe it was the burning curiosity of why I had a heat pack, or maybe it was the baffling enigma of why I looked like I was melting under the fluorescent office lights. Regardless, the result was the same: another grand reveal of my ever-misbehaving body.

Now, I know what you're thinking: *Okay, that's annoying, but no big deal. People know a little more than you want them to—so what?* And sure, in theory, that's fine. But you see, when people know too much, they start thinking they have a say in the matter. And that's when we arrive at my least favourite phrase in the world: *"Don't do that, it'll flare you up."*

Oh, Karen. Sweet, well-meaning, but ultimately misguided Karen. Just because you've witnessed my body's rebellious antics doesn't mean you have the inside scoop on how this all works. Life is not as simple as *this will flare me up* or *this won't flare me up.* Sometimes, the real question is: *Is this worth the flare-up?* Because here's the thing: sometimes it is. Example: The Sun.

Ah, the sun. That beautiful, glowing ball of Vitamin D and immediate regret. Heat and humidity are basically my kryptonite, and my medications have very clear instructions about avoiding direct sunlight. So, naturally, I went on a beach trip. Cue the chorus of *"Get out of the sun!" "You'll flare up!" "Are you crazy?"*

Yes, yes, and probably. But here's what people don't get—I already KNOW the sun is not my friend. I haven't somehow *forgotten* that it messes me up. Instead, I've run a mental cost-benefit analysis. How much fun will I have vs. how miserable will I be later? And in that moment, feeling the warm sun on my skin, enjoying the beach, and just *living*—yeah, I decided the minor flare-up was worth it.

Life isn't black and white. It's a thousand shades of grey (not the scandalous kind, unfortunately). While I appreciate the concern, only I get to decide when the risk is worth the reward.

So, dear well-meaning advisors of the world, let me live. If my lungs decide to drop the hottest album of the year mid-shift, so be it. If I choose a sunburn and a flare-up in exchange for a beautiful day at the beach, that's my call. And if I ever decide to actually keep my medical history a secret? Well... that's between me and my ever-dramatic immune system. But let's be real—I'll probably lose that battle too!

"Aww, But You're So Young" - The Age-Old Commentary

People often say, with a tone absolutely *dripping* in pity, *"Aww, but you're so young."* You know the voice—the one usually reserved for lost puppies, sad movie endings, or when someone finds out their favourite coffee shop is closing. It's the kind of reaction that makes you wonder if they expect you to suddenly burst into tears right there on the spot. I'll admit, it was worse at 15 than it is at 26. And that comment usually falls into one of two categories.

Category One: The 'You'll Grow Out of It' Club

This is where people confidently tell me, *"You're young! You'll grow out of it!"* Ah yes, because clearly, all medical conditions come with an expiration date, and I must have just missed the memo. My GP told me the same thing when they chalked everything up to *growing pains*. Hah—yeah, *about that*. Turns out, it *wasn't* growing pains, and I *definitely* didn't grow out of it. If anything, I grew *right into it*.

I remember waking up in the mornings with my hands so stiff that it took *hours* to loosen them up enough to function. I'd sit there thinking, *Why is no one else getting these 'growing pains' but me?* It was isolating, to say the least. And as a teenager, hearing *"Oh, it's just growing pains, you'll be fine"* wasn't just dismissive, it made me doubt myself. For a while, I even thought, *Maybe I'm just weaker than everyone else. Maybe I just can't handle things as well as other people can.* Spoiler alert: *nope, turns out I just had a chronic illness. Who knew?*

Category Two: The 'So... It Only Gets Worse?' Panic Club

Now that I'm an adult, the commentary has shifted. Instead of the false hope that I'll magically outgrow my condition, I get the opposite reaction: full-blown existential dread. People's eyes widen like I've just dropped some life-altering bombshell, and they ask, *"Sooo... this will just keep getting worse and worse?"* as if I've just informed them that I'm single-handedly responsible for the end of the world.

And oh, it doesn't stop there. Some people decide to turn it into an impromptu medical interrogation: *"But what happens if the meds stop working?" "If the muscles around your lungs just keep getting weaker, then what?" "Wait, so like... what's the long-term outcome here?"*

Oh, I don't know, Susan—maybe consult *literally any* medical professional instead of treating me like a one-person WebMD search engine. It's as if people assume I have all the answers when, in reality, I'm just out here winging it like everyone else. Do they really expect me to say, *"Oh wow, I hadn't considered that! I guess I should start panicking now!"*

Here's the thing: I get it. People don't always know what to say. Chronic illness isn't something everyone has experience with, and sometimes, their reactions come from a place of genuine concern. Maybe, just *maybe*, we could retire the *pity voice*, ditch the *doomsday questions*, and just, you know... *talk to me like a normal person*. At the end of the day, my life isn't some tragic countdown. It's a life. A *good* life. And trust me, I'd much rather talk about *literally anything else* than whether or not my lungs will betray me in the next decade.

As much as I would love to simply tell people to *just keep their mouths shut* when it comes to commenting on my health, I understand that some people just *can't help themselves*. So, instead of screaming into the void, I suppose I should say something *productive* for those who feel the *overwhelming* need to weigh in.

Yes, having a chronic illness from a young age means I've had it for *a longer period of my life*. But here's something that might surprise you—I'm actually *partly grateful* that I was diagnosed young. Don't get me wrong, it has had its immense challenges (because obviously), but there have also been some unexpected benefits.

I was recently talking to someone who was diagnosed with a chronic illness at the age of 34. She told me about all the ways her life had suddenly changed, how she was struggling to adjust, and how overwhelming it felt to have everything she knew suddenly shift. That's when I realised I never had to *adjust* in that same way. I mean, sure, there were changes, but for the most part, I *grew* with it. I didn't have a sudden "before and after" moment where my world flipped upside down; I just adapted as I went.

Of course, there were hard moments. Watching my friends get their driver's licenses while I had to navigate different limitations. Seeing them travel and do things I sometimes *couldn't*. But on a day-to-day level? I don't actually *remember* life without a chronic illness. It's always been part of my reality, which means I learned how to function with it from a young age.

I also picked up a lot of skills along the way: how to manage school and work while dealing with chronic pain and fatigue, how to advocate for myself in medical settings, and perhaps most importantly, how to *not* be embarrassed when I get sick in public. (Okay, that part's a *bit* of a lie—*everything* embarrasses me—but you get my point.)

At the end of the day, I'm *open* about my condition because it's been part of me for so long. It doesn't faze me. And if that surprises you—if you're one of those people who feel the need to make *big-eyed, dramatic comments* about my age—maybe just take a step back and think before you speak. Because while I appreciate the concern, I appreciate *thoughtfulness* even more.

Support, Not Solutions: Understanding Chronic Illness and Respecting Beliefs

I feel a need to slip in a little sneaky disclosure before diving into this chapter. I'm a big believer in *you do you*. People's personal beliefs—whether individual or part of a larger collective—are just that: personal. And as long as those beliefs don't start creeping into my life uninvited, by all means, you do you.

This brings us to the age-old topic of religion. Now, I know that typically, it's safer to steer clear of religion and politics, but I had a comment thrown my way at one point that really stuck with me. Someone told me, *"You need to pray more."* You know, so that I could get better.

Now, let's start with the basics—I'm not religious. I was raised Catholic, but I don't actively practice. Throughout my medical journey, I've had plenty of people telling me that they'll pray for me, and honestly? I think that's quite lovely. Religion aside, what they're really doing is taking time out of their day to do something they genuinely believe will help me, and that's a kind and thoughtful gesture. No issues there.

But when the conversation shifts from *"I will pray for you"* to *"you need to pray more, and you won't get better until you do,"* that's when we start crossing into problem territory. See, I have a lot of thoughts on this, but I won't go too deep. I think prayer is a great coping mechanism. I mean, take the well-known serenity prayer: *"God, grant me the strength to accept the things I cannot change, the courage to change the things I can, and the wisdom to know the difference."* That, to me, is what prayer can be—asking for strength, perspective, and resilience.

And if that's how someone personally navigates their struggles, then great. But here's where I draw the line: I have the wisdom to know that no amount of prayer is going to *erase* my autoimmune condition. It's not about a lack of faith or effort on my part—it's just reality. Maybe prayer helps someone cope, and maybe for some, it even brings healing in its own way. But telling me that the reason I'm not "better" is because I don't pray enough; that's not okay.

I know there may be people reading this who disagree, and that's fine—because that circles right back to my original point. No one should be telling me what I should believe in, and no one should be implying that my lack of religious devotion is the reason for my illness. Faith is a deeply personal thing, and just as I respect others' right to believe, I expect that same respect in return.

It's also just *awkward* sometimes. Like, how exactly do I respond when someone tells me, *"You just need to pray more"* or *"let's pray together so you can get better?"* Do I politely say, *"Oh no, I don't actually believe that,"* and risk watching their face fall like I just told them Santa isn't real? Or do I awkwardly nod and go along with it just to avoid the whole uncomfortable moment?

Here's the thing—I genuinely don't want to be disrespectful to someone else's beliefs. But why am *I* the one tiptoeing around their feelings when they haven't stopped to consider *mine?* Why is it suddenly my job to manage the awkwardness of rejecting something I never asked for in the first place?

Let's add another fun layer to this—the timing. Because, oh, the *timing* of these conversations. It's one thing to have this chat in a casual setting, but I've had someone drop the *"just pray and you'll be healed"* wisdom while my head was literally inside a toilet bowl, throwing up from a bad reaction to new medication. I mean, what response were they expecting in that moment? *"Oh, great point! Let me just finish vomiting and I'll get right on that."*

It just baffles me sometimes. Like, read the room. Maybe—just maybe—if someone is actively *unwell*, that's not the best time to hit them with unsolicited spiritual advice. While I respect faith and people's right to believe in whatever brings them comfort, I also respect *my own* right to say, *"No, thank you"*— without the side order of guilt or awkwardness.

If you've made it this far—congratulations! You deserve a gold star, a round of applause, or, at the very least, a snack break. Thanks for sticking with me and taking the time to understand my perspective. I know conversations like this aren't always easy, but they matter. So, if you're wondering what to do with all this newfound wisdom, let me break it down for you lightly because life is already heavy enough.

1. Respect That Everyone's Journey Is Different

Think of life like a buffet; everyone's plate looks different, and just because one person swears by the potato salad doesn't mean it's for everyone. Whether it's chronic illness, religion, or personal beliefs, no two people navigate life the same way. What brings one person comfort might not work for another, and that's okay! The best thing you can do? Listen. Just listen. Resist the urge to play life coach unless you have an actual certificate (and even then, maybe tread lightly).

2. Offer Kindness, Not Conditions

If you want to pray for someone, send good vibes, or do an interpretive dance in their honour—fantastic! But remember, support should never come with an *asterisk*. Saying, *"You need to pray more so you get better,"* is basically the equivalent of giving someone a gift and then charging them rent to keep it. If your intentions are good, let them stay that way—without sneaky conditions attached.

3. Focus On What Actually Helps

Instead of diving headfirst into a TED Talk on how someone *should* be handling their situation, try this groundbreaking, revolutionary approach: ask them. A simple *"Hey, how can I support you?"* goes a long way. Sometimes, people don't need a magical solution; they just need a person who listens, brings snacks, and doesn't start sentences with *"Have you tried...?"*

4. Understand That Some Things Are Out of Our Control

Look, if mindset alone could cure chronic illness, trust me, I'd have been healed somewhere between my 200th motivational quote and manifesting better health by drinking *one* green smoothie. But unfortunately, that's not how it works. Encouraging someone to stay strong? Great. Implying that they *could* fix everything through prayer? Nope. Just nope.

The Art of Offering Random Objects and Emotional Spiral Management

I've noticed a fascinating phenomenon: when people are out of their comfort zone and, they tend to spiral. Now, there are two primary ways this plays out. Either they start offering me completely random objects, or they descend into a full-blown panic. At this point, for some inexplicable reason, I become their emotional support human instead of the other way around.

Let's start with the offering of random items.

Picture this: I was sixteen years old, catching a flight by myself for the first time. I was heading home to Sydney after spending the school holidays with my aunt and uncle. I felt incredibly mature, ready to take on the world until about three hours into the flight when I felt the aura. A seizure was on its way.

Trying to play it cool, I turned to the random woman next to me and asked for a Panadol—because, you know, that always works. (Spoiler: it does not.) Next thing I know, boom. I wake up to an air steward aggressively rocking me back and forth like he was performing some kind of DIY CPR-meets-chaotic-lullaby routine. Shoulders to knees, back up again. Rinse and repeat.

In my groggy state, I had one clear thought: *What the heck is happening?* Gathering what little energy I had, I stopped the utterly pointless rocking, sat up, took off my oxygen mask, and reassured everyone that I was fine.

And that's when I noticed it. The entire plane was staring at me. Cue the offerings.

"Sweetheart, would you like a mint?"

"Luv, I've got some spare socks if you need them."

"Hi, I'm Bill. My daughter faints, and she drinks lemonade after. I asked the air hostess to get you one."

For a split second, I genuinely questioned whether I had hit my head. While I deeply appreciated the concern, this was my first realisation that when people don't know what to do, they just start throwing stuff at you regardless of its relevance. But hey, if people are in the mood for handing things out, I'll take a new immune system, thanks.

And then there's the other reaction. Some people, after witnessing one of my medical episodes, will lock eyes with me—the person who just went through the entire ordeal—and say something like, "I just need a moment. That was really scary for me."

"Oh, I'm sorry. Was my near-death experience inconvenient for you?" Well, now I'm being dramatic, but you get it. Cue me offering them emotional support.

Look, I get it. Watching someone struggle medically can be confronting. I don't like seeing other people in pain, either. But to the friends and family of those with chronic illnesses: please, please try to hold it together in front of us. It's already awkward enough when I'm gasping for air; it becomes exponentially worse when I have to use my last bit of energy to console you about how hard it was for you to watch me suffer.

If you need a moment, take it. But maybe take it after the person in crisis has, you know, stabilised. Go for a walk. Take some deep breaths. Cry if you need to. But do not stand there while I'm still struggling to breathe to tell me how you were affected by it.

I remember when my lungs first started getting impacted. When things got bad bad, I would get the holy trinity of respiratory drama: bronchospasm, a throat stridor, and wheezing in my lungs. A noisy, chaotic mess. Sometimes, I would be gasping for air, sweating buckets, looking (and sounding) like I had just crawled out of a disaster movie.

The majority of the time, someone would say, "Wow, that was terrifying for me to watch." And every single time, I would reply, "I'm so sorry."

WHY?! Why was I apologising? I was the one suffocating (well, not literally), yet there I was, consoling the onlookers like a therapist on the clock. So, to my fellow chronically ill folks: please don't make my mistake. Do not waste your precious energy apologising for something that is absolutely not your fault. And to the friends, family, and coworkers: like always, think before you speak.

At the end of the day, I know these reactions come with care or at least confusion. But if you're unsure what to do, let me help—stick to useful offerings. No socks, no mints, and for the love of all that is good, no panic. If you really want to help, try this: ask what I need, and then actually listen to the answer.

And if all else fails? Just bring me snacks. Snacks are always a good choice.

The Mental Health Twist

I thought I'd heard every diagnosis under the sunad enough diagnosis for a lifetime. Chronic migraines? Check. Autoimmune? Oh, absolutely. PCOS and endometriosis? You bet, I've been there. But then, life hit me with something that made even my chaotic brain go, "Wait... what?!"

Let me set the stage: it was the year everything came crashing down, or rather, everything got *dramatic*. So, in addition to the regular mental gymnastics I'd been doing for years, it was finally time for some more diagnosis. And when I say "official," I mean they dropped a *bomb* of diagnoses on me that made my head spin. Ready for this? The ADHD and autism flags are waving strong. So tThis one is still a work in progress. I've jumped through all the clinical psychology assessment hoops and have now been passed off to the psychiatrist for... well, something somethingthe final ticks and scripts. Honestly, I have no idea what comes next — I'm just hanging out in the magical land of "pending." At the moment, I'm proudly sitting on a waiting list... to find out if I can get on *another* waiting list... to *maybe* make an appointment. Yep, it's a waiting list inception. I didn't even know that was a thing, but here we are. Honestly, I'm not entirely sure what comes next, but we're waiting for that appointment. Stay tuned for the next thrilling installment of *"What's Going On in My Brain?"*

Then, as if that wasn't enough, a hefty serving of severe depression and extremely severe anxiety. And let's not forget the cherry on top: apparently, I have perfect emotional dysregulation. (At least I'm doing something perfect!)

So, does that mean I'm a walking DSM-5?" I had to laugh because what else do you do when you've been hit with a cocktail of diagnoses that sound like the plot of a psychological thriller?

But here's the twist: while I thought I'd heard it all, this year, I learned that mental health is a whole new beast. I had to get real with myself. Turns out, all these conditions don't make me a walking disaster—they make me *me*. Sure, it's a lot to juggle (trust me, I'm now carrying a mental health diagnosis arsenal in my back pocket), but it's also a little freeing. Now, when I feel overwhelmed or anxious, I know why. And when I forget to do the one thing I promised myself I would do—again—I know it's not because I'm lazy, but because my brain's wiring is a bit... let's say, creative.

So, welcome to my world: a delightful cocktail of neurodivergence and mental health highs and lows. It's not always fun, but it sure keeps life interesting. I mean, who needs a boring existence when you can have a mind that's a bit of a rollercoaster? At the end of the day, I've realised that, hey, I may have a *lot* of labels, but I'm still figuring it out. And let's face it, we're all figuring it out one day at a time. And if nothing else, I'm now *definitely* an expert ina top-tier contestant for mental health trivia.

Alright, now that we've got the diagnosis part out of the way, let's dive into the real fun: *the comments*. You know the ones. Those well-meaning but utterly *baffling* things people say when they find out you've been handed a mental health diagnosis cocktail.

Personality Preserved: The Medication Debate Continues

So, we've already had the whole *medication-is-poison* debate, right? The one where everyone seems to have an unsolicited opinion on what I should and shouldn't take, as though my body is a community project. Let's move on to the next chapter in my pill-popping saga; this one involves a little extra sprinkle of *psychological* fun. After I was diagnosed with ADHD and autism entered the scene, it was like opening a whole new can of worms. Suddenly, the conversation shifted again, but this time, people were more than willing to offer advice on *my brain*— as if it were a shared community resource.

After the tests came back, the clinical psych recommended medication to help balance out my dopamine levels—essentially topping up the "good vibes" chemicals that aren't typically abundant in my brain—and something to calm the hyperactivity I've got going on. I mean, sure, that sounds reasonable to me, but oh boy, did the comments come flooding in. First, we had the classic: *"Oh no, don't do that, you'll lose all your personality!"* Wait, what? Excuse me, but no, I will *not* lose my personality. It's not like the medication's going to swap my thoughts with some bland, robotic version of myself. It's almost comical how whenever medication and mental health are involved, everyone seems to assume that the magic pill is going to suck out all your quirks and turn you into a lifeless husk.

Here's the kicker: I hadn't even mentioned what the medication was or its purpose. But, as soon as I said *medication*, the red flags went up, the alarms sounded, and the immediate reaction was a resounding "no-no-no." It's funny (and a little infuriating) how people hear "medication" and immediately assume the worst—like it's some evil, personality-stealing potion—without any actual understanding of what the medication is for or how it works. If I mentioned that the meds would help calm my brain so I could function better, suddenly I was *going to become a robot* or *lose myself.* But if I go unmedicated, well, I'm too "hyper" or "distracted" to focus. The irony here is delicious.

It just goes to show that the stigma around mental health and medication runs deep. I'm not about to let a few uninformed opinions derail my ability to function, but I would really appreciate people taking a moment to, you know, keep their thoughts to themselves unless they have a prescription for *understanding*. Because my brain is mine—and whatever meds I take to make it work better aren't going to make me any less of who I am.

And then there's always the other classic comment: *"But you function so well without medication."* Oh, the irony. Yes, from the outside, I might seem like I've got it all together. Thanks for noticing, but here's the thing: *that's called masking*— and trust me, I'm an expert. I've had years of practice. If by "high functioning" you mean that I can navigate social situations, keep a job, and appear somewhat put-together, then sure, I guess you could say I'm high functioning. But behind that polished exterior is a whole different story. The truth is, it's an absolute struggle every single day.

What you don't see is the emotional turmoil I experience, even when I seem calm on the outside. For example instance, I can't always regulate my emotions well. If someone so much as shows a slight micro-expression—whether it's a raised eyebrow or a change in tone—that sends my brain into overdrive, thinking I've done something wrong. My mind immediately assumes that I've upset or offended them, and that triggers a full-on anxiety spiral. I get stuck in my own head, trying to decipher every little detail of their expression or behaviour to figure out what went wrong. If I misread the situation, it sends me into a cycle of self-doubt and stress, unable to focus on anything else.

Or take social interactions that don't go quite as planned. If someone expresses any sort of dislike for something I did, I can easily fall into a depressive episode. It's like a weight drops on my chest, and I spiral into negative self-talk, wondering if I'm just a walking disaster. All these emotional waves, these ups and downs, can be incredibly draining. And yet, on the outside, you'd never know. I can still show up to family gatherings, participate in conversations, or make it through a workday, all while keeping these feelings buried beneath the surface. But it's exhausting.

So, yes, I *can* keep going without medication, but *why* would I? Why should I continue to force myself to navigate life in a constant state of anxiety and emotional turmoil when there are tools and medications available that could make my day just a little bit easier? Why should I keep pretending everything is fine when I'm struggling to keep it together? And that's where the problem lies. The reason these comments even exist is that the people saying them have never experienced what it's like to go through a day in my shoes or anyone else's shoes who's managing a mental health condition. They only see the version of me that I've allowed them to see—the one that looks like I'm functioning perfectly fine like I've got it all together. But here's the truth: I don't. It's *darn hard.* It's exhausting to constantly put on a face and pretend I'm okay when I'm struggling inside to manage emotions and social cues that don't come naturally to me.

Just because I'm *able* to function doesn't mean I'm not fighting a constant internal battle. I may appear "fine," but I'm often just one small thing away from feeling completely overwhelmed. Masking takes a toll on me, mentally and emotionally. And the idea that I should just "suck it up" or "keep going" because I *can* manage without meds is a dangerous oversimplification. Medication isn't about weakness or being incapable; it's about giving me the tools to live more comfortably in my own skin. It's about making my day just a little bit easier so I don't have to expend all my energy pretending everything is okay. So, yeah, I might seem like I'm "fine," but the truth is, no one knows the full extent of what I'm managing on the inside. And I really wish people would remember that before they offer unsolicited advice on how I should be handling it.

The Art of Functioning While Freaking Out: A Journey With High-Functioning Anxiety

Oh, high-functioning anxiety. It's a term people love to throw around like it's a badge of honour, but let me tell you, it's more like a straightjacket that you're wearing while trying to climb a mountain in stilettos. Everyone loves to say, "You don't have anxiety! Look at how much you're getting done!" Or, "Your anxiety is high-functioning!" Well, thank you, Karen, for that insightful diagnosis. I'm sure the fact that I'm currently juggling eight projects while internally spiralling is *totally* proof that I've got everything under control.

But here's the real irony: high-functioning anxiety isn't some superpower where you're crushing life and drinking green smoothies while meditating on mountaintops. No, no. It's a pressure cooker with a smile on its face. It's this nervous energy that compels me to take on more than I can handle, like writing a book in my *spare* time, which is funny because I don't really have spare time. But hey, why not add a book to the mix, right? If I keep myself busy enough, I won't have to listen to my brain screaming at me about everything else that could go wrong. Spoiler alert: it doesn't work that way.

So, I overload my plate to avoid the discomfort of sitting with my thoughts, but then *the plate is too full!* And what happens when the plate is too full? Burnout. Anxiety. More tasks, because now I've already failed at keeping up with the previous ones. The cycle continues. Rinse, repeat.

But yes, I guess I am the textbook definition of "high-functioning anxiety" if we're going by the surface-level metrics of how many things I can juggle without dropping them (spoiler: I drop a lot). But let me be clear: the "functioning" part is no walk in the park. It's more like trying to run a marathon on a treadmill that's speeding up every time you take a step. You can keep going, sure, but it's exhausting and terrifying, and at some point, the treadmill is going to launch you across the room. That's how I feel most days: like I'm on a treadmill that's going faster than I can keep up with, but if I slow down, I'll fall flat on my face.

Now, let's talk about the medical stuff, because that's a whole other layer of irony I didn't sign up for. I never used to get anxious about the medical challenges. In fact, when I was having three seizures a day, I was almost... *fine* with it. You know, you get desensitised. The seizures became part of my daily routine, like a weird, unwanted alarm clock that goes off at random times. It wasn't ideal, but I'd gotten used to it. But fast forward to now, when I'm more stable on medication (thank you, modern science), and the seizures are more like a distant memory, showing up once a year, tops, you'd think that would be a good thing, right? But no; now, the idea of having another one scares the heck out of me. It's like when you get a taste of normalcy, and suddenly, the old problem seems much scarier than it ever did before. It's the fear of *what if* that kicks in. And that, my friends, is what I like to call the paradox of "high-functioning anxiety." You're juggling tasks and crushing goals, all while quietly bracing for that next round of chaos, whether physical or mental.

So, here's the thing. I fill my days with tasks to distract myself from the constant aches and pains— like my joints feeling like they've been run over by a truck or the wheezing in my lungs that makes me sound like an old vacuum cleaner. Oh, and let's not forget the migraines that show up just when I think I've got everything under control. I stay busy so I don't have to pay attention to my body's subtle (and not-so-subtle) complaints. But of course, that leads to me pushing my body to its absolute limit, which triggers another round of anxiety, which just feeds back into the cycle. It's like running on fumes but convincing yourself you're fine as long as the engine is still running.

The worst thing isn't even the physical flare-ups. The worst thing is *not* overloading my plate. Because when I'm not buried in tasks, that's when I have to face my own thoughts. And let me tell you, that's like staring into the abyss and wondering if the abyss is also judging you for not doing enough. If I'm sitting still, with nothing to distract me, I start thinking about all the things that *could* go wrong, all the things that *have* gone wrong, and the growing list of things I haven't done yet. It's a black hole of worry. So, guess what? I'd rather keep going. Keep adding more work to the pile, keep spinning plates because at least when I'm busy, I don't have time to think.

And to those people who love to say, "But it's high-functioning anxiety." Let me just say: sure, maybe my "functioning" looks great to you on the outside. But just because I'm productive doesn't mean I'm not internally a hot mess. Anxiety doesn't care about your metrics of success. It's always there, lurking, even when I'm ticking off items on my to-do list with military precision. Just because I'm *getting things done* doesn't mean I'm not fighting an internal battle the whole time.

So, yes, I am "high-functioning." But it's not as glamorous as it sounds. It's exhausting, it's stressful, and sometimes, it feels like I'm sprinting toward the edge of a cliff while telling myself, "It's fine, everything's fine." But I keep going because the alternative is far worse. So here I am—high-functioning, task-obsessed, perpetually anxious, and yet somehow still making it through.

Would You Rather: An Autoimmune Disease or Autism? A Life-Altering Game Show

And just to tie everything together, there's always that one person who loves to ask the big reflective question. You know, the type, the kind, that looks at your life and then, without prompt, dissects the part they think is the most "shitty." They'll look at you, ponder for a moment, and then throw out something that makes you question whether you should laugh, cry, or both. One time, for example, someone casually asked me, *"Would you rather have lupus your autoimmune disease or autism?"*

That was a tough one, seriously! I remember hearing that and just sort of giggled awkwardly because, well, people pleaser, over here, didn't want to rock the boat. But in the back of my mind, I was floored. I should've said something, but at that moment, I didn't have the words. What I wanted to ask was: *Why would you think it's okay to ask that? Why would you pit these two things against each other as if one is worse than the other?*

The truth is, both my autoimmune disease and autism are part of my story, and both have shaped me into who I am. And neither of them is inherently negative, even if the world sometimes wants to paint them that way. Autism gave me a unique way of looking at the world through a very specific lens, and, yes, an occasionally awkward and overly literal perspective. My autoimmune disease, on the other hand, taught me patience and resilience. It gave me the strength to keep moving forward despite my body's constant attempts to derail me. So, while I may be fighting an uphill battle with both conditions, I've also gained skills that many of the so-called "healthies" don't have. I've learned how to adapt, to push through adversity, and to achieve the same things that others do—but with a few more hurdles along the way.

It's like trying to kayak against a strong tide: every stroke takes more effort, but with every push against the current, you build more strength. Eventually, you reach the same place that someone else paddling in calm waters reaches. The journey is harder, yes, but it makes you stronger. And in the end, that strength is something no one can take away from you. I've had to adapt in ways that others never will. I've learned to recognise the value of my unique perspective to see my struggles as part of a larger narrative that isn't defined by what I can't do but by what I can overcome.

I won't pretend that autism and lupus chronic illness don't come with their challenges. Yes, sometimes my *tism*—as I like to call it—can land me in some truly awkward situations. I misread social cues. I have difficulty understanding nuances in conversation. I might say the wrong thing at the wrong time. But those quirks, while they may cause some discomfort, are part of who I am. They don't make me any less of a person; in fact, they make me more authentic. I've learned to love my weirdness because it's mine, and it's what makes me, well, *me.* That awkwardness is what gives me personality; it's the thing that allows me to laugh at myself and see the humour in moments that others might take too seriously. It's the same quality that lets me connect with others who feel like outsiders, who are trying to navigate a world that wasn't built for them.

So, to anyone who's just been diagnosed with something that feels like it's going to be the hardest thing to live with—whether it's autism, chronic illnesslupus, or something else entirely—please hear me when I say: don't let people create your narrative for you. Don't let them define your experience. It's so easy for others to look at us from the outside, to see our struggles and assume they know what our lives are like. But they don't. They see the version of us that we've allowed them to see. The one that looks like it's all put together. The one that makes it look like we're fine, even when we're not.

But the reality is, *we're allowed to be more than our struggles*. We're allowed to build our own story, one that includes our challenges but also celebrates our resilience. I've learned that while life may throw a lot of curveballs my way, I get to decide how to respond. I get to create my own narrative that says, "Yes, this is hard. But I'm still going to fight, still going to show up, and still going to do the things that matter to me."

And yes, I'll probably keep being awkward. I'll misread some cues, I'll say the wrong thing at times, and I'll probably make some people uncomfortable along the way. But that's okay. Because I'm learning to embrace who I am, quirks and all. And I promise, the journey—no matter how hard—is worth it. So, for all of you out there, whether you're newly diagnosed or you've been living with these challenges for years, take a moment to remind yourself: You are *not* your diagnosis. You are so much more. And your narrative is yours to write, not anyone else's to dictate. Embrace it. Own it. Because at the end of the day, you're the one paddling, and the strength you build along the way is what will get you to the place you want to be.

"Don't Let It Define You"–Unless It Does: A Guide to Surviving Well-Meaning (But Totally Misguided) Comments About Autism

Ah, the classic: "Yeah, you have it, but don't make autism your whole personality." I've heard this one more time than I care to count, and honestly, I didn't expect it to come up nearly as often as it has. But, here we are.

Let me break it down: growing up, there were definitely struggles—especially socially. I always felt a bit out of sync, like I missed the memo on how to properly "fit in." As I got older, I finally got the diagnosis that explained so many of the things I'd struggled with. The social awkwardness, the sensory overload, the need for routine—suddenly, it all made sense. It was like someone handed me a map to a place I'd been wandering around for years, but never quite understood how to navigate.

So, as I started to figure out *why* I was the way I was, I also began to open up to people about it. I'd explain, "This is why I do things this way" or "this is why I get overwhelmed." I thought it might help people understand me better and maybe even be more patient with me. But, nope. Enter the classic well-meaning but deeply frustrating comments: "Yeah, but you don't need to let it define you" or "don't focus on it so much."

Now, I get what they were trying to say; they were trying to be supportive, I guess, but let me tell you, nothing feels more disempowering than someone telling you *not* to focus on something that has been your reality for your entire life. It's like saying, "Don't focus on that huge, gnawing toothache—you don't need to make it your whole personality." Oh, really? Because it kind of *is* my reality, whether I like it or not.

Let me give you a little example of how this all plays out. Once a year, my family (and sometimes the extended family from my mom's side, which, trust me, is *a lot*) goes on a family holiday. Now, let me tell you, this is nothing short of a sensory minefield. Picture it: A big, loud, Italian family, all together in one place. The noise, the constant overstimulation, the endless opinions, the inevitable changes in routine, the lighting that's too bright, and the unfamiliar bed with the scratchy sheets that I swear were designed by someone who hates sleep. It's a lot.

So, I get there, already feeling like walking on a tightrope, trying to keep my cool and not snap at anyone because *that's* the thing I don't want to do—make a scene. I'm already on edge, trying to manage all the sensory overload and avoid the meltdowns that sometimes come with it. Then, after a while, I start to get overwhelmed and mention my new autism diagnosis to a few people in the family. And what do I hear? "Yeah, but don't let it define you."

I'm like, *really?* First of all, I didn't go around defining myself by my diagnosis until you started making me feel like it was a thing I needed to hide. Second, the diagnosis didn't change my life the way you think it did. Here's the thing that most people don't get: for many of us, getting the diagnosis doesn't suddenly add new struggles or *reveal* new symptoms; it's more like a giant "Aha!" moment that explains the things we've always felt. The struggles were already there. The overwhelm was already there. The social difficulties were already there.

So, when I add a label, it's not like I'm suddenly becoming more *affected* by my condition. It's more like I'm finally able to see the puzzle pieces fit together. The diagnosis doesn't create new challenges; it helps me understand the ones I've had all along. And that's the thing people often miss. The diagnosis doesn't change me; it just gives me the tools to better understand myself.

So, yeah, I'm not going to "not focus on it" or pretend it doesn't shape my experience—it's been a part of me for my whole life. And the sooner people realise that the sooner they can stop offering those well-meaning but ultimately unhelpful comments. Thanks, but no thanks.

I totally get why people around me react the way they do. For them, it's like they've been seeing me one way for so long, and then *bam*—suddenly, I drop a diagnosis on them. They're like, "Wait, this is new?" But here's the thing: for me, it's not new at all. The diagnosis just gives a name to what's always been there.

See, when I spend so much of my time masking— hiding parts of myself to fit in or make others comfortable—people don't see what's going on underneath the surface. They don't see how much energy I'm spending just trying to manage social interactions. So, for them, the diagnosis might feel like it's coming out of left field. They might worry I'm going to overthink it or dwell on it too much, and that's why they tell me, "Don't let it define you," or "don't focus on it too much." They just don't get that it's been a part of me for as long as they've known me. The only difference now is that I finally have the words to explain it.

Instead of rushing to give advice or brush it off, what I really need (and what we all need) is for people to take a step back and ask a simple question: *Did you suspect this?* Ask me how I've been feeling, what I've been struggling with, and—most importantly—*listen.* It's not just about the label; it's about understanding the context of my life and how I've experienced the world. The diagnosis didn't change who I am; it just gave me the language to talk about it more openly.

Don't assume you know what's going on. Don't just tell me not to dwell or overthink it. Take a moment to ask, understand, and maybe even learn something new about me. Because, for me, this diagnosis is just another chapter in a book I've been writing for a long time—it's not a plot twist.

"Resting Bitch Face, Overactive Heart: The Empathy Misunderstanding"

Another classic: "You're not empathetic." I'll tell you, this one really gets me. When I was married, my now ex-husband would often tell me I wasn't empathetic—usually during a heated debate, which, let's be honest, is *never* the best time to throw that kind of criticism around. So, naturally, I didn't exactly take it to heart. Debates can get fiery, right? You don't always trust the words flying in the heat of the moment. But fast forward about a year after my separation, and guess what? A friend casually dropped the same bombshell on me. And, of course, because it was so familiar, I briefly entertained the thought. *Maybe I really am a heartless robot* until my defensive switch flipped, and I went straight into full-blown "No way, not me!" mode.

Here's the thing, though: I consider myself to be *overly* empathetic. Like, I could probably enter the "Empath Hall of Fame" if that were a thing. I feel *everything*. When someone opens up about their emotions, their struggles, or their experience, I *take it in*. And when I say "take it in," I mean it like a sponge at maximum saturation. Their feelings, their pain, their joy—it all becomes my own. I *absorb* it. It's like emotional osmosis. So, how on earth could anyone look at me and say, "You're not empathetic"? The nerve! I'm practically drowning in other people's emotions over here, and yet, I'm the one being accused of not feeling?

Then, it hit me. The issue wasn't that I wasn't empathetic—no, no, that was all there. It was that the external signals weren't matching up with what I was feeling internally. My face, you see, often betrays me. My "resting bitch face," as it's lovingly referred to, could easily be mistaken for indifference or coldness. My facial expressions tend to default to a neutral (or, okay, let's be honest, slightly unamused) look, even when I'm internally *bursting* with empathy. So, while inside, I might be feeling a tidal wave of sympathy for someone, on the outside, I just look like I'm plotting my next great act of villainy.

It doesn't stop there, folks. I recently explained to someone that I am, in fact, highly empathetic, and I'm sorry if it's not coming through clearly—it's just that my face doesn't do what my heart is doing. You'd think that would clear things up, right? Nope. Apparently, that wasn't good enough either. I was told that I needed to "meet people halfway" and make more of an effort to show it. *Oh, I see.* So, in addition to being an emotional sponge, I now have to also become a professional facial contortionist? Got it.

Here's the kicker, though: if you're someone who's neurodivergent, your brain works a little differently. We don't always have the same instinctual cues as neurotypical people. Sometimes, I'm so focused on processing the emotions in the conversation that I forget to put on the appropriate facial expression. Or maybe I'm just processing at a different pace. By the time I've caught up emotionally, I might look like I'm mentally checking out. But just because my facial expression isn't matching up with what's going on inside doesn't mean I'm not there with you.

So, yeah, meet me halfway. Understand that neurodivergent brains don't always work the same way as neurotypical ones. We process emotions, expressions, and social cues differently, and we're *trying.* We're not robots, even if it sometimes seems like we are. It would be nice if the world could cut us a little slack, stop assuming we're cold or detached, and maybe try to understand what's really going on under the surface. I swear, I'm more empathetic than 90% of the people I know—I'm just working with a different emotional toolkit, and unfortunately, my face didn't come with a user manual.

The "You Don't Seem Autistic" Chronicles Continued

Ah, the joys of being open about having ADHD and autism. You'd think, in this day and age, people would just nod, say, "Oh, cool," and move on with their lives. But no. Instead, one of the most *hilarious* responses I've encountered is: *"I don't think so."*

Oh. Ohhhhhh. Well, silly me! Here I was, thinking that six hours of rigorous assessments with a qualified professional might mean something. Turns out, Karen—who sees me once a year at a family BBQ and whose main credential is having an opinion on *everything*—is actually the real authority on neurodivergence. My bad.

What exactly am I supposed to say to that? *"Oh, must be a misdiagnosis, then! I'll just return my autism card at the door."* I mean, on what basis is this expert analysis even made? Is it my eye contact? My ability to hold a conversation? The fact that I don't fit whatever stereotype you have in your head?

I even once tried to counter with, *"Well, I did six hours of assessments..."* thinking that might, you know, add some weight to the whole "this is real" thing. But no. The response? *"Yeah, but everyone's on the spectrum."*

So... wait. Do I *not* have it, or do I suddenly *definitely* have it? If you're going to have a wildly unnecessary opinion, at least *commit* to it.

It's almost as if people think they're paying me some kind of compliment by saying, *"I don't think you have it."* But spoiler alert: *it's not a compliment.* It's dismissive. It invalidates years of struggling with things I didn't have the words for, only to finally get answers and be told, *"Nah, doesn't seem right to me."*

At first, I made the rookie mistake of trying to explain. I'd list all the little quirks, all the signs that led to my diagnosis, hoping for some sort of lightbulb moment where they'd go, *"Ohhh, I see it now."* But then I realised something revolutionary: *someone else's lack of understanding of an issue is a "them" problem, not a "me" problem.*

It's funny because these same people don't tend to apply the same logic elsewhere. No one looks at someone with a broken leg in a cast and says, *"I don't think so. You don't really seem like you have a broken leg."* Or questions about someone's asthma diagnosis because they saw them walk up a flight of stairs without collapsing. But when it comes to neurodivergence? Suddenly, everyone's a part-time diagnostic expert.

And let's not forget the classic follow-up: *"But you seem so normal!"* Ah, yes. My Oscar-worthy masking skills, honed over years of trying to function in a world that doesn't cater to me. Thank you for acknowledging my performance. I'd like to thank my hyper-awareness, my internalised anxiety, and society's unrealistic expectations. Without them, this convincing display of "normalcy" wouldn't be possible.

Then, of course, there's the well-meaning but completely misguided comparison game. *"Oh, my friend's kid is autistic, and they can't talk. You're not like that, so you must not be autistic."* Right. Because autism is one single, identical experience for everyone. That's like saying, *"Oh, my friend has diabetes, and they take insulin. You don't, so you must not have diabetes."* Make it make sense.

At the end of the day, I've learned to save my energy. If someone wants to believe their uninformed opinion carries more weight than a professional diagnosis, that's their personal side quest. I no longer feel the need to justify my existence, and I certainly don't need validation from

Karen at the family BBQ.

So, to anyone who feels the need to share their completely unqualified opinion about someone else's diagnosis: maybe just... don't. And if you really must, at least be consistent. Nothing is more exhausting than trying to follow a logic train that derails every two seconds.

Meanwhile, I'll be over here, thriving in my *actually diagnosed* neurodivergent glory. And if you don't think I have ADHD or autism? That's fine. Just know that the next time I hyperfocus on an obscure topic for six hours straight, forget to eat, or get overwhelmed by the existence of fluorescent lights, I'll be thinking about you, Karen. And laughing.

Final Thoughts

Look, I hope this is all making you chuckle a little. But just to clarify: this isn't me recounting some list of ridiculous comments for the sake of a good laugh. No, no, no. This is a lesson for you. So, listen up. The next time you feel like offering up your "wisdom" about my health or anyone else's, how about you zip it? We don't need your unsolicited diagnosis or your comedic interpretations of *our* chronic illness.

Remember, some things are better left unsaid. And if you can't figure that out? Well, you might just be one of the reasons I keep a mental list of "things not to say." You're welcome!

So, to all the people who can't keep their mouths shut, I hope this demonstrates the impact of your words. For the most part, I just smile and nod along. I've gotten pretty good at it over the years. I go through phases where I just grin and bear it, sometimes even giggling at the absurdity of it all. But let's be real—sometimes, those comments end in tears.

I know I'm not the only one out there with chronic health conditions who has had to endure the strange, insensitive, and downright hurtful things people say. So many of us feel the weight of these words, even if we don't always show it.

The first day I passed out in the halls of H Block at high school, waiting for the bus, I wish someone could have pulled me aside and told me what was really coming. I wish they'd said, "Yes, it'll be painful. Yes, it'll be challenging. Yes, it'll be a little tricky dealing with health complications. But the hardest part? The hardest part will be the shit everyone says." It won't be the flare-ups, the medication side effects, or the endless doctor appointments. It'll be the unsolicited advice, the comments, the well-meaning but utterly clueless things people say; those words will stick with you. But somehow, you *have* to find a way to smile, nod, and keep going. And in the end, that'll be your real superpower.

I'm confident that there are countless others who share similar experiences. For them, I want to say: you're not alone. We're all just trying to live our lives despite the things that are said to us. And we'll keep pushing forward, no matter how many people feel the need to offer their "helpful" opinions. Because, in the end, we are more than the sum of the comments we've received.

To the Newly Diagnosed

To the people recently diagnosed with chronic health conditions, welcome to the party. Buckle up because you've got a lifetime of comments, questions, and unsolicited advice ahead of you. Now, you have two choices going forward:

You can try to educate everyone around you, patiently explaining how things really are, the science behind your condition, why it's not a phase, and why you're not exaggerating. You can spend hours fielding questions like, "Have you tried that thing I saw on the internet?" or "are you sure it's not just stress?" You might even give a TED Talk at some point on the real experience of living with a chronic illness.

OR

You can just smile and nod. This option is very underrated but incredibly effective. Someone says, "You look fine, are you sure you're sick?" Smile, nod, and move on with your life. Someone tells you, "Have you tried essential oils?" Just smile, nod, and then quietly Google "how to politely ignore people who suggest essential oils" on your phone.

The thing is, you can try to educate everyone, or you can choose to save your energy for important matters. Either way, you've got this. Seriously. You are now equipped to handle a lot—physical challenges, emotional roller coasters, and the endless parade of unsolicited advice. You're going to do it with grace (or at least, with a well-timed side-eye).

So, welcome to the world of chronic illness. You might not have asked for it, but it's yours now. And hey, you'll probably find a pretty awesome sense of humour along the way. Honestly, I'll leave that choice up to you. Either way, you've got this.

So, if you know me—or even if you don't—and you have someone in your life dealing with an autoimmune or chronic illness, just because your gems of wisdom aren't in here, don't go patting yourself on the back just yet. Like I said before, some of the most outrageously ridiculous comments got left out, all in the name of peacekeeping. Trust me, it's for the greater good.

If you're reading this and happen to recognise something you've said or done in the past, please don't take this as a personal dig; it's not aimed at you. What I'm trying to do here is create some awareness. A lot of people like me—people-pleasers at heart—tend to smile, nod, and keep quiet, even when what's being said has a negative impact. We don't always speak up, partly because we're so focused on making others feel comfortable or avoiding conflict, that we let those comments slide, even if they hurt.

But the thing is, we internalise a lot of those comments, and they can build up over time. It's not that we don't appreciate the good intentions behind them, but sometimes they can feel a bit dismissive or even invalidating. The truth is, most of the time, we're just trying to get through the day, and the last thing we want is to make someone feel bad, so we stay quiet. But this is a chance to open up that conversation and help people understand that sometimes those well-meaning words have a deeper effect than expected.

This isn't about pointing fingers; it's just about starting a dialogue so that we can all be more mindful of how we interact with others, especially when it comes to sensitive topics. It's not easy for people like me to say, "Hey, that comment stung." We might not always express it in the moment, but it's important to be aware of the impact we can have on one another—whether we intend to or not.

So, here we are—at the end of this book but,

realistically, not anywhere close to the end of the journey. If life has taught me anything, it's that there's *always* another plot twist waiting around the corner. Whether it's a new diagnosis, a surprise hospital stay, or just another delightful encounter with the medical system (*shoutout to the doctor who once told me to "just think of something I want to open my eyes to"*), the story never really stops. And maybe that's the point.

I started writing this because I wanted to put into words what it's like to navigate a body that treats existence like a constant science experiment. I wanted to document the absurdity, the frustrations, the small victories, and—most importantly—the humour in it all. Because if there's one thing I've learned, it's that laughter makes even the most ridiculous, unfair, and exhausting moments a little easier to bear.

I've spent years trying to figure out how to live in this body, how to advocate for myself, and how to balance resilience with rest. And through it all, I've learned that the key isn't about fighting to be *normal*; it's about making peace with the chaos. It's about finding your people, naming your struggles (literally, in my case), and realising that you don't owe anyone an explanation for how you feel.

So, if you're reading this because you, too, are navigating the unpredictable, the misunderstood, the exhausting reality of chronic illness, know this: you are not alone. Your experience is valid. And most importantly, you don't have to be *inspirational* every damn day just to make other people comfortable with your reality. If nothing else, I hope this book made you feel a little more seen. Or, at the very least, gave you a laugh at Albert, Stacy, Terry, and the rest of the uninvited guests crashing my body.

Now, if you'll excuse me, I need to go argue with Stacy about why we *really* don't need to cry over running out of soy milk.

And to the people around me: please, by all means, keep the absurd comments coming. After all, material for a second book isn't going to write itself. *Or... and hear me out... you could just zip it.* Your call.

ABOUT THE AUTHOR

Marie has spent years navigating both the ups and downs of life with health challenges. She has turned her experiences into a lighthearted yet insightful exploration of the strange and often ridiculous things people say when they don't understand chronic illness. With her sharp wit and relatable storytelling, Marie's writing not only entertains but also offers support to those who may feel isolated by their conditions while providing families and friends a window into the sometimes confounding world of chronic illness.